She shall be called

Abigail

A Widow's Story of God's Love

PAM EDDINGS

She Shall Be Called Abigail
A Widow's Story of God's Love

By: Pam Eddings

ISBN-13: 978-1985132351
ISBN-10: 1985132354

All scripture quotations in this book are from the Authorized King James Version of the Bible unless otherwise noted.

Edited by Cindy Moore

For information, to schedule speaking events, or to order books by Pam Eddings, please communicate by email to **eddingspam@gmail.com.**

FOLLOW ME on TWITTER: pameddings

FRIEND ME on FACEBOOK: Pam Eddings

Table of Contents

Dedication

To:

My Lord Jesus, who has been with me every step of my journey
through these long years of widowhood.

My sons and their families
Russell, Ashley, Kevin, Ryder, and Molly
Raymond, Desiree, Bethany, Kristen, and Sophia
Rodney and Jazmin
For your unfailing love, and support.

All the widows in my immediate family.
Kathryn Nixon, Donna Nixon Best, and Imagene Eddings
I honor you for remaining steadfast in your faith.

Every widow who has blazed the trail before me and taught me how to
persevere and accept my new reality by trusting myself to the loving
hands of my Lord and Savior, Jesus Christ.

Acknowledgements

When I decided to begin putting this book together, I remembered a remark made in passing last year by my friend, *Cindy Moore,* when she said she had majored in English in college and enjoyed working with words. I called her and discussed my idea for the book and the seemingly impossible task of putting it together in under two weeks. She was willing to take on the task of editing as I wrote.

We went to work, and the text messages and phone calls were frequent as files continued to be exchanged in our shared Dropbox folder. She challenged me to express how I was feeling at certain points in my journey. Her insightful comments for keeping my focus on the purpose of the book kept me on track. I could not have done this so quickly without her expert help. Thanks a million, *Cindy.*

Leslie Greenbank has been walking the path of widowhood for several years. Her story is in this book. When I would get stuck, she would call and suggest that I consider adding this idea or that article. She wrote a superb article about her experience with the physical manifestations of grief after her husband died. If is included in the Appendix. Thanks, *Leslie* for your contributions.

Since so much of my story involved my children and grandchildren, I was constantly emailing files to them for their input. They expressed their approval and support again and again. Text messages were exchanged to help me remember cute little things the grandchildren would say or do. This is not only my story, but it is also the story of how all our family has coped with the loss of husband, father, father-in-law, and grandfather. Thanks for your love and support, *Russell and Ashley, Raymond and Desiree, and Rodney and Jazmin.* You and my wonderful grands have given me reason to live and thrive. I love you all so much.

This project consumed me once I started and I would sometimes forget to eat or take a break from the computer. My dear friend, *Linda Thomson,* would check in daily and ask, "Have you eaten?" "Are you taking breaks?" Thanks, *Linda,* for helping me to be the best I can be.

Thanks to all the *Abigails* who were willing to share some portion of their story in this book. Your triumphs have been an inspiration to me.

And to everyone else who allowed me to clear my schedule and get this burning message into the world, I give my sincere thanks.

Foreword

Tokens of Pam's Love

Giving
By: Cindy Moore

Give, and it shall be given unto you; good measure, pressed down, and shaken together, and running over, shall men give into your bosom. For with the same measure that ye mete withal it shall be measured to you again. Luke 6:38

You have heard it said that you cannot out-give God. In all the time I have known Pam Eddings, I do not know of a more giving person. We often think about giving in monetary terms, but it goes much deeper than that. I know Pam as a diligent, hard-working, committed, and caring woman. She gives of herself by ministering to others through Bible study, speaking engagements, music, and authoring books. She gives of herself in love, friendship, and encouragement. She gives of her time, traveling for her calling; her talent, with music and teaching instruction; her gifts of writing books and editing; and her resources, having given away dozens of her books and even proceeds from sales. Everything she does is for the benefit of someone else whether it is a church, a family member, a friend, or a stranger. Many people think of tithing 10% to the work of God and giving a little more for an offering. Pam does what is required and then goes above and beyond in offering herself. I know she has doubtless been a spiritual inspiration to many others as indeed she has been to me. I thank God for using her and pray God gives her blessings as her heart desires because I know her primary desire is for His Kingdom. I appreciate my friend, Pam, whom I've known since childhood, for giving of herself to be the spiritual leader God has called her to be.

Introduction

A friend approached me after church in the summer of 2017 to tell me that God had given him a message for me during the night. He said, "When you were married to Ron, you were like Jacob's wife, Rachel, in the Bible. You were very loved, cherished, and provided for. After Ron died, God became your lover, friend, provider, and protector as well as anything else you needed. He changed your name to *Abigail* which means, *the Father's joy*. Now, God wants you to write a new book and share the story of His great love and provision for you during your journey down the road of widowhood. This book will be an encouragement to many other widows who are struggling with their identity and provision of daily needs. During these years of being a widow, God has taken great joy in providing for you, His Abigail, and restoring your joy. You've got to share your story!"

Through the years, many people have asked me to write my story, but I have been reluctant to relive the early days of my loss and put the words on a page. In addition, I did not know how to convey my experiences in a way that would bring hope and healing to others who had experienced the death of a spouse. I am certain God's time had not arrived until now.

On January 23, 2018, God began dropping ideas into my mind for this story. Since then, the ideas have continued to flow with a sense of urgency. With God's inspiration and the help of many others, this book has come together more quickly than I expected it could. You are holding the results of that inspiration in your hands. I pray it will bring comfort and healing, and restore joy, hope, peace, and laughter again.

In Jesus' Name!

Pam Eddings

February, 2018

> *I will instruct thee and teach thee in the way which thou shalt go:*
> *I will guide thee with mine eye.*
> **Psalms 32:8**

The Rachel Years

God Brings Two People Together

Move to Colorado

Ron Eddings, a native of Springfield, Missouri, was the oldest of five boys in his family. His dad, Rev. James Eddings, felt in prayer that God wanted him to plant a new Pentecostal church in Boulder, Colorado. He answered that call in August, 1957 when the family sold their home in Springfield, loaded everything in a moving van, and relocated in Boulder. Ron graduated from Boulder High School in May, 1968 and enrolled in Colorado School of Mines in Golden, Colorado that fall. His father resigned the Boulder church in the summer of 1969 to accept the pastorate of a church in Mountain Home, Arkansas. Ron's parents and four brothers moved to Arkansas, leaving him in Colorado to continue his schooling.

~~~~~

I was born in Lake Charles, Louisiana to Hubert and Gloria Nixon and am the oldest of five children in my family. My dad worked for Southern Bell Telephone Company, and his job required frequent moves across south Louisiana during the early years of my life. When I was in the fourth grade, we settled in the small town of DeRidder, Louisiana and lived there almost six years. Then, in early 1968, my dad had a dream about our family moving to Boulder, Colorado. Although our family had vacationed in Colorado several times, we had never visited Boulder. A decision was made to include Boulder in the family vacation that summer. Because I was involved in Bible quizzing that year and had a tournament scheduled during vacation time, I opted to remain home with my grandparents. My two sisters also stayed with me.

During that vacation, my parents attended the church in Boulder that had been founded by Rev. James Eddings. James was out of town that weekend, but Imagene Eddings invited my parents and brothers to eat lunch with her and her five boys after church.

After returning home from Boulder, my parents discussed a potential move with our pastor, Rev. V. A. Guidroz. After much prayer concerning the matter, Daddy applied for a job transfer to Boulder. They told him if he had not received an answer in six months, he would need to apply again. We had sold our home and lived in a rental home for a year. When the transfer did not come through, our pastor suggested that perhaps God wanted us to remain in DeRidder and be a missions supporter with our prayers and finances. So, we purchased a new home and had only been in the home six weeks when the transfer was granted. We concluded that God wanted us to go, so we put our home in the hands of a Realtor. (It took about a year for it to sell.) We then contacted Ron's dad to tell him of our decision to move to Boulder, and he gave us Ron's contact information.

We packed everything again over the Christmas holidays and left our beautiful home on January 1, 1970 to move to Boulder. Upon our arrival, we were greeted with deep snow on the ground and extremely cold temperatures which we were unaccustomed to experiencing in south Louisiana.

My first meeting with Ron Eddings occurred on the day we arrived at our rental home when he and his uncle, Roger Hale, met us and helped us unload the moving van. I was a fourteen-year-old freshman in high school, and Ron was a twenty-year-old sophomore in college.

Ron's fondest memory of that day occurred after the van was completely unloaded, and we all met back inside the house to visit for a few minutes. My spinet piano had been placed in the hallway until we could decide

where to put it. My mother mentioned that I played the piano and asked me to play something for Ron and Roger. My piano teacher and pastor's wife, Sis.[1] Robbie Guidroz, had taught me how to add flare to my music. I had used her guidance to create

---

[1] Ephesians 3:14-15 refers to the Church as being members of the family of God. Since we are family, we refer to each other as brothers and sisters in Christ. It is especially respectful to address ministers, leaders, and elders with the title Bro. or Sis. before their first or last name.

my own version of the song "Poor Rich Man," and that is what I played for Ron and Roger that day. Ron often referred back to that moment as the day the pretty little girl from Louisiana serenaded him on the piano with "Poor Rich Man."

Friendship Blossoms into Romance

Because Ron's family was in Arkansas, he spent much time with my family on the weekends when he was not in school. He enjoyed my mother's spicy southern cooking. We didn't have a dishwasher in those days, so my sister and I were responsible for doing dishes after we ate. Often Ron would take my sister's place in the kitchen and dry dishes while I washed so we could have more time to talk with each other.

During the winter, we went on outings to the mountains and learned to ice skate on frozen ponds. Several of us would pile onto huge toboggans and slide down steep, snow-covered hills. In the summer, we headed to the mountains for hiking and picnics. Estes Park was nearby as well as Rocky Mountain National Park. Ron was an avid tennis player, and he often played tennis with my brothers.

In spite of the age difference, Ron and I soon learned that we shared many interests in common. One of those mutual interests was a love of music. I played piano and alto saxophone, and he played alto saxophone. We both loved to sing, and I even taught him to sing harmony when we sang together. After I became old enough to date, we often attended gospel music concerts together.

Our mutual love for God and His Word allowed us to enjoy many conversations about the Bible and its teachings. Additionally, we were both involved in teaching Sunday School at our church.

The Proposal

Ron graduated from Colorado School of Mines in May, 1972 with a Bachelor's Degree in Metallurgical Engineering[2].

[2] Metallurgy is the science of working with metals and alloys for usage in products for consumers and manufacturers.

One week after my seventeenth birthday in September, 1972, he proposed to me, and I happily accepted. I had taken extra classes during my sophomore and junior years so I could graduate a semester early in my senior year.

We set a date for December 31, 1972 and began making wedding plans. Sadly, the U.S. Army had other plans for Ron. He had received deferments from the draft during his years of college, but when he graduated, they called his number in October 1972, and he left for the Army in November, 1972.

All wedding plans had to be put on hold until Ron could finish his basic and advanced training and get approved for some leave time. During his absence, I continued working as a sales clerk at Woolco Department Store and saving every penny I could save for our wedding.

Once the date was learned for completion of Ron's training, we set a new wedding date of April 3, 1973. The mail carriers were busy transporting our daily letters to each other during the five months we were apart. Since pay phones were a little expensive to use, and cell phones were not commonly available in those days, Ron would give me the number of a pay phone in his area, and we would arrange a time for me to call him on the pay phone once a week. I would pay my parents for the phone calls when the bills came in each month.

The Wedding

The wedding week finally arrived. Ron graduated from Advanced

Training as a Medic and received his assignment for duty in the hospital at Ft. Ben Harrison in Indianapolis, Indiana. He arrived in town four days before the wedding. Our house was overflowing with out-of-town family, including both of my grandmothers and one grandfather as well as my cousin, Dana, who was one of my bridesmaids. Ron's family also came in from Arkansas and stayed in a hotel.

Because there were four younger siblings in my family, Ron and I did not want to put any unnecessary financial hardship on my parents to pay for a wedding. I made my dress and borrowed a veil from my Aunt Rachel. All my attendants made their dresses, and I made ties for each of the groomsmen to match the dress of the bridesmaid they escorted. I also made Ron's tie. We paid for the live flowers we used as well as the photographer. My parents paid for the simple reception which included cake, punch, and nuts. The beautiful cake was made by a lady in our church, who discounted her service as a gift to us.

The wedding was beautiful. I sang to Ron, and two of our brothers played a trumpet duet for one of the songs. Our car was hidden at the Denver airport, and a co-worker of my mother snatched us away from anyone who wanted to follow us when we left. A couple in our church gave us the gift of a few days in their cabin in the mountains of the Big Thompson Canyon.

During our honeymoon, we drove to Boulder one day to take care of getting my name changed on my driver's license, social security card, and bank account. While we were in town, it started snowing, and we could not get back to the cabin to get our clothes. Mr. Lafferty went up and got everything for us and left it at my pastor's home in Denver. The roads were icy on the day that we drove to Denver to get our things. We arrived safely at the Parker's home, but on our return to Boulder, our car slid off the road as we merged onto the highway. No damage was done, but we had to wait until a wrecker arrived to pull us out of the snowbank. Meanwhile, the policeman called my dad to tell him his son-in-law had been involved in an accident. At first my dad denied that he had a son-in-law. We had only been married a few days, and he had not gotten used to the idea of having a son-in-law. We spent the last two days of our honeymoon with my family.

All too soon, the honeymoon was over, and we loaded our car with the wedding gifts and my personal items. As we traveled from Colorado to Indiana, we stopped in Arkansas for a few days to visit Ron's family. We then drove to Indianapolis to begin our new life together. Within a couple of days, we had purchased a used mobile home and had it moved to a lot in the Ft. Harrison mobile home park.

Family Years

Indianapolis, Indiana

We found a small church near Ft. Harrison and became involved there as Sunday School teachers. The building only had two rooms and a bathroom, so on nice weather days, Ron and I brought a table and chairs outside, and we conducted class in the church yard. I played organ and started a small choir. Ron and I often played saxophone duets in church and sang together. The church grew and built a beautiful new church on several acres nearby.

Ron was discharged from the U.S. Army in November 1974 and immediately accepted a position as a Metallurgical Engineer in the research lab at FMC in Indianapolis. We moved our mobile home to a park nearer to Ron's work.

Our first son, Russell, was born in March, 1976. My parents took vacation from work and spent a week with us to welcome their first grandchild into the family.

Shreveport, Louisiana

Shortly after Russell was born, we decided to relocate closer to our families. We researched several states to find companies that would need a Metallurgist. We sent out fifty letters and resumes, and received responses from five companies in three states requesting an interview. After scheduling the interviews, we took a trip to attend the interviews. Ron received offers from three of the companies. After reviewing the offers, he accepted an offer from Beaird-Poulan Weedeater in Shreveport, Louisiana. We sold our mobile home and moved to Shreveport in September, 1976. This relocation situated us almost halfway between my family in Baton Rouge and Ron's family in Mountain Home.

After a short stay in an apartment, we purchased a home in south Shreveport on a large wooded lot. We visited area churches and chose one for our home church. As was our custom, we became involved in teaching Sunday School. I played piano in church, and Ron played his sax. In time, we also served as youth leaders with another couple in the church.

During our five years in Shreveport, we added two more sons to our family. Raymond was born in January, 1978, and Rodney completed our family in July, 1981.

Our time in Shreveport gave Ron the opportunity to fulfill a dream of becoming an airplane pilot. He received his private license and used his GI benefits to study for an advanced certification. We were able to rent a small plane, and the GI benefits paid 90% of the rental costs. Because it was so inexpensive to fly, we took frequent trips to Mountain Home and Baton Rouge to visit our families. We even flew cross-country in 1980 to San Diego, California to visit family. Upon our return home, Ron's GI benefits were completed, and we never flew again.

Hendersonville, North Carolina

In 1980, Beard-Poulan began making plans to relocate the factory to Nashville, Arkansas. They offered all employees the opportunity to remain with the company and relocate with them. Ron visited Nashville and decided he was not interested in moving our family there. He engaged a professional job search agency and requested another job in Shreveport. Additionally, since we had vacationed once in the Smokey Mountains and had fallen in love with North Carolina, he also told the agency we would consider a job in western North Carolina. We prayed for God's direction, and an opportunity presented itself near Asheville, North Carolina with Rockwell International. A new factory was being built to manufacture axles for large trucks, and Ron was hired to set up the heat-treat

department. He oversaw the purchase of all the furnaces and equipment and organized the department.

We moved to the small community of Hendersonville, North Carolina in February, 1982. Our boys were ages six, four, and six months. We spent a couple months in a log cabin on a lake.

22

After looking at many houses, we finally decided to buy land and build. We purchased eleven acres on top of a mountain, and Ron drew the plans to build our dream home. We left the log cabin and rented a house for one year while we built. Ron's dad, in addition to being a great preacher, was also a master builder. He agreed to come out and stay with us for most of that year to help us build our new home. We also had expert help along the way from other family members as we needed them. We moved into our mountaintop retreat in April, 1983.

While living in the rental house during the year of building our house, I began to seek the Lord about ways to meet people. I had been an avid coupon clipper in Shreveport, so I decided to place an ad in the newspaper to meet other ladies who clipped coupons. About a dozen ladies responded to my ad, and I scheduled a time for them to meet in my home with the coupons they couldn't use. While getting acquainted, we put our unneeded coupons in a box and passed it around, taking what we could use out of the box. I continued meeting with these ladies periodically for several years. In time, God opened doors for me to teach home Bible studies to several of them. Several years later, one of those families became part of our church, and one of their children participated in Bible Quizzing with our boys.

When the boys were in Elementary School, I spent time each week volunteering in their classes. Sometimes I tutored a student in reading or math. One year, I taught a weekly music class to fifth graders.

I became involved with the Parent-Teacher Organization. The President appointed me as devotional chairman one year. It was my responsibility to invite someone to share a devotion and prayer at the meeting or present one myself. In those days, public speaking was not my area of preference, so I chose others to present all the devotions except for one time. For that particular occasion, I made up a tune for Philippians 4:8 and taught my son's class to sing it. The students sang that verse as part of the devotion, and I chose another person to pray. From devotional chairman, I was appointed to serve as Vice President of the PTO. I agreed to accept only if I didn't have to do any speaking. I was assured that no speaking was required unless the President could not attend. Wouldn't you know that the President's husband got a job transfer mid-way through the year, and the position of President fell on me. With lots of instruction in protocol for leading meetings, I managed to get through the remainder of the school year. Even then, God was preparing me for my future calling of teaching and ministering in public.

During our fifteen years in North Carolina, we experienced wonderful memories of camping, hiking, and picnics in the Blue Ridge Mountains. Our acreage was surrounded with one hundred acres of woods, and our boys explored every part of it and built treehouses and rock forts all over the land. It was a great place to raise a family.

Church involvement continued to be a major part of our lives. We drove a long distance for many years and served our church in music, Sunday School, and Bible quiz coaching. Ron also served as trustee, and I served as church secretary. Our boys also became involved in music and Bible quizzing.

Russell graduated from high school and eventually moved to Springfield, Missouri to learn construction from an uncle who owned a drywall business. Raymond graduated from high school and moved to Raleigh, North Carolina to attend North Carolina State University.

Glenwood, Iowa

In early 1997, Ron received a phone call from a professional job search agency asking him if he would be interested in a job opportunity with Eaton Corporation in Shenandoah, Iowa. Ron listened to their description of the job and expressed interest in looking into it. He flew to Iowa for an interview, and the company paid for a second trip for Ron, Rodney, and me to spend some time in the area. After discussion and prayer, Ron accepted the offer, and he moved to Glenwood, Iowa shortly afterward to begin the new position. Because Rodney was still in school, he and I remained in North Carolina until school was out.

As part of our relocation package, Eaton had rented and furnished a two-bedroom apartment for Ron when he moved. They also provided a moving company to come and pack everything in our North Carolina home and put it into storage until we purchased another home in Glenwood. Meanwhile, we put a contract on a large home that was being built. Although we only had one son still at home, we viewed the house purchase as an investment. We remained in the apartment until the home was completed. After we moved in, several family members helped us finish the basement, which added to the equity in our home. We had a fifteen-year mortgage on it and a fairly large monthly note. Our intent was to enjoy it during Ron's employment with Eaton Corporation and sell it when he retired.

When Ron accepted the position with Eaton, his goal was to remain there for five years, at which time he would be vested in their retirement program. Then we planned to spend one year on the foreign missions field as AIMers.[3] After the missions term was completed, we planned to retire in Springfield, Missouri.

In preparation for the goal of becoming AIMers, we decided to celebrate our twenty-fifth wedding anniversary with a visit to see life-long friends and missionaries, Darrell and Cindy Collins in Bolivia, South America. We arrived in Cochabamba, Bolivia in February 1999. During our two-week stay, we visited several cities and churches in the country. Darrell would tell the church people that we were coming back in two years to work with

them. The people would clap and tell us in their limited English that we were welcome in their country. We came home with the assurance that a year of missions work was compatible with our dream. This photo was taken during a Sunday morning worship service in Tarija, Bolivia. I was trying to sing from the Spanish songbook.

Rodney had finished his senior year a semester early, so he spent the two weeks we were in Bolivia with his oldest brother, Russell, in Springfield, Missouri. During his visit, he decided he would like to stay and attend college there. He proceeded to get a job, and by the time we returned home, he was happily settled in Springfield. I was sorry to see him leave since he was the last son at home. However, life continued on without him.

Once all the boys were out of the house, I went to work part-time in a real estate office as a secretary for all the agents. Employees in our office were expected to attend various civic events. During my two years in that office, I became acquainted with most of the city officials, Realtors, bankers,

---

[3] AIM (Associates in Missions) is a program of the United Pentecostal Church, International in which a person does short-term missionary work to assist a full-time missionary in whatever area they need assistance.

attorneys, pastors of local churches, Chamber of Commerce members, and other business men and women in Glenwood. The broker in our real estate office expressed interested in a Bible study, so I went to work an hour early once a week to teach her. My friendship with our State Farm agent also resulted in a weekly Bible study during her lunch hour.

In 1998 one of my neighbors introduced me to a neighborhood Bible study that had been in existence for over fifty years. People from various denominations would gather and study the Bible chapter by chapter each week. They had studied through the entire Bible many times over the years. I began attending the meetings and inviting people to my church. Several of the ladies and a few men even consented to letting me teach a Bible study in their home. Ron and I also hosted a weekly Bible study in our home for interested people in the community.

By 1999, several people from this group had been baptized in Jesus' name and filled with the Holy Ghost. The church we attended in Nebraska was twenty-five or more miles away from most of the people we were teaching. A decision was made by our pastor to sponsor a new church in our area. A young minister, Alan Poe and his family, Dujuana, Cherith, and Adena were chosen to be the pastor of the new work. Initially, we rented a church and held Sunday and Wednesday evening services there. In time, we reserved a meeting room at a bank in Glenwood and met there. Of course there was no music in the room, so we had to bring my heavy keyboard and set it up for every service. Finally, we moved to another church in the

 community of Bartlett and kept the same schedule. Over the course of two years, we had seen approximately thirty people baptized in Jesus name and filled with the Holy Ghost. This is a picture of our little group one Wednesday night during a visit by missionaries, Richard and Coral Denny.

One day in the fall of 2000, Ron called me at work to inform me that he was bringing Mark, a newly hired man at Eaton, to look at our home and see if he would be interested in purchasing it. I was surprised and responded that our home wasn't for sale. Ron said, "Mark has been looking at other homes in our neighborhood, and I told him if he liked our neighborhood, he would really like our home. Besides, I've been praying that when God is ready for us to unload this large home, He will send a buyer to us without us having to list the home with a Realtor."

That night, Mark came to our home and liked what he saw. A week later he brought his wife, and they immediately signed a contract to purchase our home.

We immediately began packing and searching for a place to live. God provided a nice brick rental home in Glenwood that we were able to rent without signing a lease. My parents came to visit us for Thanksgiving 2000, and they helped us get everything moved and settled into our new home.

God had sold our large home without us having to list it with an agent and had provided a rental home without a lease. Little did I know that six weeks later, Ron would be gone. If I had been left with that house and its huge monthly note, I would not have been able to make the payments with the income I earned as a part-time receptionist in a real estate office. But God knew, and He had provided for the sale of our home in advance. The money was in the bank and available for my next home purchase, the one I would make after I moved to Springfield, Missouri.

Ron's final service in the little church in Bartlett, Iowa was Wednesday, January 17, 2001. I was playing the piano as he led worship. In between songs, he stopped and with tears streaming down his face, he told a story about a young girl he had met one summer at Arkansas youth camp after his parents moved to Arkansas. She was the daughter of influential business people in the state and was a very gifted singer. She sang throughout the week at camp. In time she married and began traveling with a gospel music group. This path eventually led her away from her heritage. He further told us this Gospel message that Jesus died to provide for us was the most precious treasure we had in life, and he did not ever want anything to enter his life to lead him away from the Gospel that had been given him. Little did he know that he was leading his final worship service and pleading with those present to hold tightly to the Truths they had been taught. His passionate plea continues to replay in my mind and keep me holding tightly to the unchanging teachings of God's Word.

Tokens of a Husband's Love

Affirmation

Let thy fountain be blessed: and rejoice with the wife of thy youth. - Proverbs 5:18

Ron took great delight in paying me compliments for my achievements. When I was in college, I studied classical music. He had become accustomed to hearing me play church music when I would sit down at the piano. However, once I started studying the classics, he would periodically ask me to play classical music while he sat in his recliner and listened. Then he would tell me how beautifully I played.

Another area where I received frequent affirmation from Ron was in the area of sewing. I had made most all of my clothes since I had taken sewing in high school. Before that, my mother had made most of my clothes. After we married, I frequently made him ties to match my church dresses. We also had several matching tops. One day he said he would like for us to have matching tailored suits. I had made a lined, tailored suit with bound button holes when I was in high school, but I had never attempted something as difficult as a man's suit. But since he believed I could do it, we went to the fabric store and picked out patterns, fabric for the suits and lining, and the required notions. Ron selected a plaid fabric, and he wanted every plaid to match. I knew that would be a huge task. However, he helped me. We laid out the yards and yards of fabric on the carpet in our living room and proceeded to pin front and back sides of the fabric together, making sure the plaids on the top matched the plaids on the bottom. Then he helped me lay out all the pattern pieces for both suits, again making sure that all the adjoining pieces were cut in such a way that plaids would match when sewn together. We cut the pattern pieces, and I proceeded to sew. Both suits turned out beautifully. I even had enough leftover scraps to make vests and pants for Russell and Raymond when they were ages four and two. We had a family picture taken with the four of us in our matching suits. After that first attempt at making a man's suit, I made two more suit jackets for Ron in later years. Of course, he selected plaid material both times, and of course, I matched every plaid. With a husband who loved affirming my achievements, I felt like I could accomplish anything. Writing about these memories sure makes me miss him. It also makes me realize the value of a compliment to raise one's self-esteem. It's encouraging to know someone believes in you.

Giving

…remember the words of the Lord Jesus, how he said, It is more blessed to give than to receive. – Acts 20:35

Ron took great delight in giving to Kingdom needs as he became aware of them. Many times we would be sitting in a church service and a need would be presented. He would look at me and ask me to get out the checkbook. I would immediately think of an amount to give because I was more familiar with what was in our account. When I would ask how much he wanted to give, his amount was always more than my amount. He was one of the most generous people I have ever met.

Not only was Ron generous in giving to Kingdom needs, but he also delighted in giving to his family, and most especially to his wife. His gifts to me in the early years of our marriage were practical things such as a leaf rake, garbage disposal, or a broom and mop. In the latter years after the boys were out of the house, his gifts became more romantic. Flowers arrived for special occasions or just because. Little cards and notes expressing his love for me were frequently given.

Ron continually reminded our boys of how special I was. He instilled in them the principle that their mother deserved the very best they could give her. When my birthday or Mother's Day came, Ron would tell me to make a list of what I would like. He and the boys would go shopping with the list. Not only would they buy everything on the list, but they would also add other things they thought I would like.

Evidently Ron's teaching to our boys was so ingrained in them that the first Christmas after his death, my boys asked me to make a list. I knew they did not have a lot of financial resources, so I made a list of three inexpensive items. True to their training, the boys bought everything on the list and added several other items they thought I would like.

After my move to Springfield, Rodney returned home to live with me while he finished college. Remembering his dad's legacy of giving, he would occasionally leave a vase of flowers on the kitchen counter for me to find when I woke up the next morning. The note with the flowers would say something to the effect of remembering that his dad used to give me flowers, so he had brought me some to remind me how much he loved me. What a beautiful legacy that *great man*, Ron Eddings, left to our family!

Unselfish

Husbands, love your wives, even as Christ also loved the church, and gave himself for it; So ought men to love their wives as their own bodies. He that loveth his wife loveth himself. - Ephesians 5:25, 28

Ron was a great example of that type of love. He worked hard to provide for our family, and willingly gave up things he wanted or enjoyed so that he could provide for the desires of other members of the family. When I decided that I wanted to go to college, he sold his big tractor and all its accessories to provide the money for my tuition. Women who receive that kind of love from their husbands feel safe in their marriage.

Financial Provision

Let the husband render unto the wife due benevolence: and likewise also the wife unto the husband. – 1 Corinthians 7:3

The dictionary defines benevolence as a desire to help or do good things for others; show kindness to someone. The Bible instructs both husband and wife to do good and be kind to each other. Ron took these teachings seriously. During the entire time of our marriage, he worked hard to provide financially for me and the boys. It was a mutual way of living for both of us. I appreciated his hard work and desire for me to be a stay-at-home mother for our children, so I tried to be careful with his earnings and spend frugally. I clipped coupons and shopped sales. I made most of my clothes and many of my sons' clothes when they were young.

While building our house in North Carolina, several unforeseen expenses occurred. A huge rock that the dozer couldn't move had to be blasted out of the basement area. We had budgeted for a two hundred foot deep well which was standard in the neighborhood, but ours ended up being over four hundred feet deep. These and other unforeseen expenses dug into our construction account. To compensate, I cut grocery and household expenses to the bare minimum in order to add to the funds in the construction account. We ate lots of pinto beans and potatoes meals during that year. His careful planning ahead has continued to take care of me even in his absence.

Ron's benevolent acts toward me did not always have a monetary value attached. Sometimes they came in the form of service. Near the end of my pregnancy with our first son, I was miserable and having difficulty resting. Even housework was extremely exhausting. One night I left him at home while I went to church to attend a baby shower for me. I had not washed the dishes in a couple of days. When I returned home, all the dishes were washed, dried, and put away. That kind of love gives security to a marriage.

Protection

Where no counsel is, the people fall: but in the multitude of counsellors there is safety. – Proverbs 11:14

There was a time when Ron protected me from losing a very valuable friendship because of an overly zealous act on my part. I had been having an extended Bible conversation with some friends on a particular topic. (I have since forgotten the topic of the conversation.) They were preparing to make a decision that was against scriptural teaching. I proceeded to search what the Bible had to say on the subject, and I wrote them a letter outlining scriptures to show why they were making the wrong decision. I added some of my own commentary in the letter. I did not discuss it with Ron until AFTER I had taken the letter to the Post Office and dropped it in the box in the parking lot. Later that evening, I discussed the topic with Ron and shared my findings in the Bible. I told him my friends needed to have that information so they could make a scriptural decision. He wisely said it was not my place at that time to push that information on them as it would more than likely destroy our friendship. I didn't dare tell him that I had already mailed the letter.

Fortunately for me, I had dropped the letter into the mailbox on the weekend, and it was not brought inside the Post Office until Monday morning. On Monday morning, I hurried to the small Post Office as soon as it opened. I knew all the employees by name there. I told the lady that I had dropped a letter into the box that was not supposed to be mailed and I wondered if she could retrieve it and give it back to me. She promptly went back and looked through the mail from the box. Thankfully, she found it and handed it to me. From that day forward, I trusted Ron's judgment and never attempted to do something like that again.

Companionship

Let thy fountain be blessed: and rejoice with the wife of thy youth. – Proverbs 5:18

Even though Ron and I were married almost twenty-eight years before his death, we never lost our delight in spending time together. After Rodney left home, it felt like we were on a continual date. Sometimes Ron would call me at work and say, "Let's go on a date tonight." He would either meet me at work or at home, and we would find a restaurant to enjoy a leisurely meal while we discussed the events of our day.

Our favorite time of the day was the evening time between supper and bedtime. We would retire to our recliners and talk about our day, Sometimes I would read to him, or turn on some of our favorite music to play in the background while we talked. Ron liked to stay informed about current events, so if he had not finished reading the paper before we ate supper, he would finish it after supper while I did needlework. I enjoyed cross-stitch, embroidery, and crocheting. We didn't have to be talking to feel that sense of companionship. Just being together in the same room was enough.

From the very beginning of our marriage, Ron let me know that his mother had prepared a dessert for the family every day. I also learned that cake and cookie mixes were not acceptable. To please him, I learned to bake his favorite cakes, pies, cookies, and other desserts from scratch. I must admit they tasted so much better than the boxed or frozen versions I had learned to prepare before marriage. Daily desserts served in the evening as *bed snacks* became a tradition in our family. Ron also enjoyed a daily glass of Pepsi with his *bed snack*.

Since Ron's death, these evening chats have been replaced with morning visits with my Lord as I read His Word and listen for Him to give me direction for my day.

Laughter

…he that is of a merry heart hath a continual feast. – Proverbs 15:15

One of the best surprises I received after marrying Ron was the gift of his sense of humor. During our three-year friendship before marriage, he was serious more often than not. I tend to be more serious-natured also, so his lack of joking and silliness was just fine with me.

However, once we were married, he showed me how to laugh and enjoy life even when times were tough. He would often take my comments very literal. For example, if I said I needed to run to the store to get a few things, he would tell me it would be more convenient to drive.

On the day of my eighteenth birthday, Ron got up before me and said he wanted to make my breakfast and serve it to me in bed. I dutifully remained in the bedroom and waited to see what he would bring to me. It seemed to take a very long time, but he finally arrived with a tray containing toast and a glass of milk. I guess I didn't have any birthday candles in the house, so he had tightly rolled up eighteen pieces of newspaper into little sticks and stuck them into the bread. He handed me the tray and proceeded to light the newspaper sticks. You can imagine the scene as they quickly burst into flames that I could not blow out. We both got a good laugh out of his first attempt to serve me breakfast in bed. In later years after the boys came along, Ron and the boys would buy doughnuts or pastries to serve me in bed on birthdays and Mother's Day.

Sometimes I tended to be moody, but Ron had a way of making remarks that would lighten the heaviness and bring a smile back to my face. One such time occurred during a church banquet. I had worn a floor length skirt and it wasn't until we finished eating, and I turned my chair around to see the speaker, that I noticed I had worn one black shoe and one navy shoe. I looked at Ron in panic and was ready to leave right then. He tried to make me laugh about it, but I was trying to hide my feet the remainder of the evening. You can be assured that we were one of the first couples out the door when the program ended. From that day forward, Ron would play jokes on me by purposely mismatching my shoes, hoping I would repeat the mistake of wearing two different colors again.

Our three sons were also gifts who brought much laughter into our home. Our firstborn son, Russell was such a happy baby. If Ron would just bounce a ball in front of him, he would burst out in contagious giggling that made us laugh with him. Now that Ron is gone, my grown sons, daughters-in-law, and grandchildren are the gifts God has given me to keep laughter in my life.

Correction

Obey them that have the rule over you, and submit yourselves: for they watch for your souls, as they that must give account, that they may do it with joy, and not with grief: for that is unprofitable for you. – Hebrews 13:17

Ron and I were passionate about teaching God's Word to our children, and Bible Quizzing was one of the avenues we used to facilitate that process. One afternoon while living in North Carolina, I packed suitcases in preparation for an out-of-town Bible quizzing tournament so we would be ready to leave when Ron got home from work. When he arrived, we started loading the car. He and I got into an argument over something that I have since forgotten. What I have never forgotten though, is the godly way in which Ron handled the situation. The boys were already outside as Ron took my hand and led me back upstairs to our living room. Still holding my hand, we knelt in front of our couch and he began asking God to forgive us and let a right spirit be manifested between us. At first, I was still pouting, but his tears and repentance melted my anger, and I too joined in with my own tears of repentance and request for forgiveness. After prayer, we hugged each other and reaffirmed our love for each other. Then we met the boys at the car and left for our trip.

During the first couple years we lived in Iowa, Ron and I taught together in the high school Sunday School class. There were a couple of sisters in our class who occasionally disagreed with some of the things we said. Word would get back to their mother, and I would receive a phone call. These conversations became tense over time, and it became increasingly difficult for me to get along with this mother. Eventually, our wise pastor decided it was time to resolve the tensions. He scheduled an evening for Ron and me, and the other couple to join him and his wife at a local restaurant. At first it was a little uncomfortable to sit across the table from this lady. Our kind pastor gently explained to all four of us that as leaders in the church, we needed to get along and be an example to others, showing the beauty of love for one another. He prayed for us. That prayer melted away all the resentment toward my sister in Christ. As we ate together, we were able to enjoy sweet fellowship with our pastor and his wife. Even though our husbands were not involved in the dispute, they provided the support we ladies needed to work out our differences and work together for the Kingdom. From that day forward, this lady and I became great friends, and that friendship continues to this day.

Opportunities for Growth and Improvement

Hear instruction, and be wise, and refuse it not. – Proverbs 8:33

Music training. In 1986 I had the responsibility of leading all the music in our church. I started a small choir which eventually grew to over thirty members. I also worked with children's music, youth choir, a small nine-member chorale, and arranged music for our church orchestra. In addition, I worked to promote singers' involvement in solos, duets, and trios. Ron's encouragement that I enroll in college for music study in 1984 had greatly enhanced my piano skills and knowledge of music theory. In 1990, I saw an advertisement about the National Music Ministry Conference in Jackson, Mississippi. After discussion about costs and time away from family, it was decided that I should attend to learn some new choir music and other tips for being more effective in music ministry. I continued attending these annual meetings for ten years.

Although Ron was very supportive of these yearly get-aways to improve my music ministry, I was equally aware of my responsibility to ensure that everything at home ran smoothly for Ron and the boys during my absence. I would spend time in advance of my trips planning and preparing menus that could be heated easily. I would leave a typed list on the refrigerator with detailed instructions about preparing each day's menu. I also arranged Ron's clothes in the closet in the order that he should wear them by putting a piece of masking tape on the collar of his shirts with the day written on it. On one occasion over the years, Ron forgot to remove the masking tape from his collar. During a meeting at work, someone asked him why he had tape on his collar. He laughingly explained our custom of me laying out his clothes for work each day.

Kindermusik. During a class at the Jackson Music Ministry Conference in 1996, I learned about the Kindermusik program for children. I brought home the information I received, and Ron and I discussed adding the certification to teach it to my credentials so I could add it to my private music instruction business. The training and teaching materials were a little pricey, but Ron never flinched at helping me rearrange items in the budget to be able to afford this new opportunity. I became certified and enjoyed teaching this program to children for several years.

The Abigail Years

January 18, 2001

This cool Thursday in Glenwood, Iowa began like any other ordinary weekday in our lives. I got up, did my devotions, and laid out Ron's clothes before going to the kitchen to prepare his lunch and breakfast for the road. After getting dressed, he came into the kitchen to give me a quick hug and kiss and tell me he loved me before heading out the door to work. As I handed him his breakfast and lunch, I told him I loved him and have a good day.

Because we had only been in this house for six weeks, I spent my morning unpacking more boxes and organizing this smaller house. My afternoon was spent teaching my little children and their mothers our final Kindermusik class of the series. After class was over, I gave the mothers a date to start the next class.

Ron arrived home from work shortly after my Kindermusik class, so I prepared a quick supper of soup and grilled cheese sandwiches. Our evening was spent perusing our photo album from our 1999 trip to Bolivia, reminiscing about our trip and dreaming of the day in the very near future when we would be on our way to spend a year assisting Darrell and Cindy Collins as associate missionaries.

We then decided to do a little exercise before heading for bed, so we went into the room containing our treadmill and exercycle. Ron got on the treadmill, and I got on the bike. He programmed the treadmill for a pretty difficult walk that involved raising and lowering the walking path and increasing and decreasing the speed of the walk. We carried on conversation while he walked, and I rode. I completed my two miles before his walk was over, so I left the room and took my shower, then went to the kitchen to load the dishwasher.

10:00 pm

"Pam!"

I stopped working in the kitchen and came swiftly to the bedroom in response to Ron's call.

"Would you pray for me? I have some strange tingling in my fingers."

I prayed a brief prayer and went back to the kitchen. A few minutes later, Ron called me back to the bedroom. This time he asked me to call the pastor who was our overseer in establishing the "daughter" church in Glenwood, Iowa. Pastor Poe recommended calling the hospital in Omaha, Nebraska for instructions. After a brief conversation with the doctor on call, Ron was advised to come in to the hospital (a 45-minute drive). They also urged him to call 911 to make them aware of our emergency.

Ron made the call to 911, but refused their offer to transport him to the hospital. He said that his wife could drive him to the hospital. I laid out his clothes, then went into the large walk-in closet to select something for myself.

Suddenly, I heard a loud crash! I came flying out of the closet and found Ron lying face down on the floor, fully dressed, with his hands at his sides. I tripped when I got to him and gashed my knee. As blood came pouring from my knee, I bent over to turn Ron's head. Blood came pouring from his nose onto the carpet.

I wiped blood from my knee and Ron's nose. I immediately called 911 and explained that we had just talked with them a few minutes earlier, but now I had a real emergency. The operator asked if Ron was breathing, and I told her I thought so because of the gurgling sounds coming from his mouth. She kept talking with me as I finished dressing and unlocked the front door so the emergency personnel could enter the house.

The emergency team arrived within five minutes and immediately began attempts to revive Ron. I was sent from the room, unaware of what was going on with my dear Ron.

Brett, a fireman from our church, lived nearby, so I called him and explained our emergency. I needed the comfort of a familiar face. He immediately came over and went to the bedroom to observe the attempts to revive Ron. Once the decision had been made to take Ron to the hospital in Council Bluffs, Brett drove me to the hospital where we were met by Pastors Anthony and Poe and their wives.

After what seemed like a very LONG wait, a very serious-looking lady came to the waiting room and told me they had done everything they could to revive my husband, but he was gone.

I was STUNNED!!! He was not sick. There was no warning. How could this be??? My nicely-ordered world had suddenly been turned upside-down. How could I go on without him? What about our ministry together in our daughter work? What about our plans to spend a year in Bolivia as associate missionaries? How would I pay these medical bills? How would I finance my youngest son's remaining college? How would I provide for my future? So many questions swirled through my head, but I had no answers. "*Our*" world had suddenly become just "*my*" world.

Although I was totally unprepared for the life-changing events of January 18, 2001, God was not unprepared. He had been preparing circumstances for my help and survival for months prior to that day, but I didn't see or understand it at the time.

When the hospital nurse told me that Ron was gone, I was allowed to go into the room where he was lying on a bed. Pastor and Sis. Anthony, Pastor and Sis. Poe, and Brett accompanied me into the room. He looked so peaceful. Surely he was only sleeping. I was convinced that if I could only touch him and pray for him, God would raise him from the dead, and he would go back home with me. I put one hand on his shoulder and raised my other hand as I immediately began praying in the Spirit. Everyone in the room joined me in prayer. The atmosphere was charged with the sweet presence of God. After a while, the prayer ended, but he did not wake up.

After the hospital paperwork was completed and my good-byes to Ron had been said, Sis. Poe drove me back home. Pastor and Sis. Anthony followed us to my house, and Bro.[4] Poe also came over after taking Brett home. The four of them spent the entire night with me so I didn't have to be alone on that first night without Ron. Sis. Anthony and Sis. Poe carefully cleaned the blood off the carpet in my bedroom. They also made coffee and kept snacks available for munching throughout the night. I spent the night in my recliner in the living room, but none of us really slept that night.

I kept replaying in my mind the scene of the hospital room and my prayer... and God's amazing presence. Wasn't God supposed to answer my prayer and send Ron home with me? I finally told Sis. Anthony that I must not have enough power for God to grant my prayer to raise Ron back

---

[4] Ephesians 3:14-15 refers to the Church as being members of the family of God. Since we are family, we refer to each other as brothers and sisters in Christ. It is especially respectful to address ministers, leaders, and elders with the title Bro. or Sis. before their first or last name.

to life. She looked at me with compassion and said, "Girl, if anyone has power with God, you do. Don't let this situation hinder your faith and trust. Evidently God had other plans for Ron and you."

Bro. Poe made a phone call to my brother-in-law, Pastor Larry Eddings, in Springfield, Missouri, who then alerted other family members of Ron's death. Larry, my in-laws, James and Imagene Eddings, and my oldest and youngest sons, Russell and Rodney, drove through the night in order to arrive in Glenwood around 8:00 am on Friday morning, January 19. My middle son, Raymond, flew in from Virginia and arrived about noon that Friday.

My sister, Paula, a pastor's wife in south Louisiana, left her responsibilities at home to fly in and help me. She arrived on the same flight as Raymond. She immediately took charge of my household by organizing the food brought in, taking all phone calls, and keeping a log of every call received and a record of everyone who brought food or gifts. She also gave my boys a prepaid long distance phone card and told them to use it to call me often.

The Funeral and Move to Springfield, Missouri

On Friday morning, my two sons and in-laws went with me to meet the funeral director. Because we wanted to have a visitation for our church family and friends in Iowa and the funeral and burial in Missouri, there were additional decisions and expenses involved in getting everything arranged. I am very thankful for Larry's guidance in helping me make all the funeral arrangements. My sons also helped me make some of the decisions. My brothers-in-law, in honor of their brother, paid for extra amenities such as limo service for the family's transport from the funeral service to the cemetery.

The first visitation was held on Saturday in Council Bluffs, Iowa. I was amazed at the number of people who came from our Nebraska and Iowa churches, Ron's work, and several of the local Kindermusik teachers. We had only been in the area for four years, but Ron had definitely impacted hundreds of people in the area.

We drove to Springfield, Missouri on Sunday, met with a local funeral director on Monday, and the second visitation was held Monday evening. Again, dozens of friends and relatives came to show their respect that evening. Our former pastor from South Carolina came with a group of people from the church and another friend from Michigan flew in for the funeral.

The boys and I had our picture taken before leaving for the service. The funeral home chapel was completely full on Tuesday morning when the funeral was held. The plant manager and another man from Eaton came to show respect. Songs were sung by Ron's cousins and my sisters and brother. Pastor Anthony read the obituary and mentioned Ron's reverence for God in his prayers by always addressing the Lord as his King. Four of Ron's brothers shared memories, and Larry preached a beautiful message about a "Great Man." One statement that remains in my memory was that Ron had experienced many hurtful challenges in his life, but he had never allowed them to make him *bitter*. Instead, the challenges made him *better*. After the service, Ron was laid to rest in the peaceful family cemetery in Rogersville, Missouri.

My parents drove from Baton Rouge to Missouri for the funeral. Afterward Paula and my parents returned to Iowa with me. Paula remained for three weeks, and my parents spent the next six weeks helping me dismantle my home and repack everything for the move to Missouri. My close friend, Judy from North Carolina, flew in and spent a week helping my parents with sorting and packing my things. I was entirely too distraught to make decisions on what to pack and what to leave behind. I am so thankful for caring family and friends who assisted me during this time.

When the news of Ron's death became known in the community, I was flooded with phone calls, cards, food, flowers and money. People we only knew slightly were so kind during those early days of my loss. I had only lived in that house for six weeks before Ron died, but even neighbors that I had not yet met, came to express their condolences and offer assistance if I needed anything.

The Cruise

Ron and I had planned to take a short three-day cruise out of Los Angeles in February. After the funeral, I called the travel agent who had booked our cruise and explained that my husband had died and I wanted to change his ticket to my son's name. They were very rude and said I could go alone, but they would not change Ron's ticket. We wrote letters and made numerous phone calls. We finally got our U.S. Representative from Missouri involved, and he took the request all the way to the top official of the travel agency. They finally relented and said they would add my son's name if I paid an additional $200. The airlines were very accommodating about changing the ticket to Russell's name.

44

The weather was cold and icy the day we flew out of Omaha. We arrived the evening before our cruise, and settled in at a hotel near the docks. We cruised to Baja California in Mexico on our second day and spent the day exploring the port area. The entire trip was bittersweet, but Russell was very attentive and tried to help me have a good time.

Finding an attorney to settle Ron's estate.

Although I was involved in all our financial and legal affairs, it was Ron who did the research and made decisions on new matters as they came up. Now I was faced with the giant task of settling his estate, arranging for moving and storing of things until I got settled again, changing names on bank accounts, insurance policies and a whole host of other legal matters. Who could I trust to assist me in making decisions on all these matters? God did not fail me in this area either.

Dewayne, one of the Realtors from my office, came to visit one day. I just happened to mention my need for an honest attorney to help me settle the estate. He told me that his son was an attorney who specialized in settling estates. He said he would ask him to call me and instruct him to take very good care of me.

Dewayne's son, Trent, called me that evening and arranged to meet my son, Raymond and me at his office the following day, Saturday morning, to discuss the process of settling Ron's estate. He told me what kinds of paperwork I needed to bring to the meeting. Over the next seven months, I met with Trent a number of times, made phone calls, and sent emails when I had questions. He was always very understanding and kind. When I finally received the bill for his services, it was much less than I had expected. Trent explained that his company had a set fee for settling an estate, whereas many law firms charged a percentage of the estate. My chance comment to my co-worker, Dewayne, had resulted in another blessing from God by directing me to an attorney who took good care of my needs for a reasonable price.

Moving again.

I had only been in the rental house in Glenwood for six weeks when Ron died. I wanted to continue our church work, but I did not want to stay in the house alone. Since I had not been required to sign a lease on the house, I could leave at any time with only a month's notice. I consulted with Pastor and Sis. Anthony for guidance. They offered me the use of the basement in their home for as long as I wanted to stay in the area, but eventually I decided that I needed the comfort of my sons, and I made the decision to move to Springfield, Missouri.

Once the decision to move was made, my brother-in-law, Mike, stepped in and told me he would handle all of my moving and expenses, including the rental of storage units for all my things until I bought another house. He arranged to bring two moving vans from Missouri to Iowa along with several family members and friends to help with loading the vans and driving back to Missouri.

The day of the move was cold and rainy. I had fretted about the whole process, but Mike told me that my job was to "sit in the recliner, sip a Pepsi, and tell everyone what to do."

The moving crew arrived in the evening and got everything loaded in a few hours. They spread sleeping bags throughout the house and everyone got a few hours of sleep. Early the next morning, I said my goodbyes to Iowa and set out for Springfield. My son, Russell, drove my car, which was loaded with items that would not be placed in storage. My parents followed in their car.

We were blessed with an uneventful journey other than driving through rain part of the way. Upon our arrival in Springfield, a beautiful rainbow lit up the sky before us. My brother-in-law, Tom quickly radioed me that God was smiling upon my arrival in Missouri. The first stop was at a storage facility to unload the vans. Mike had rented a climate controlled unit for my piano, organ and filing cabinets and another unit for everything else. My mother had organized and numbered all the boxes as they were packed, and even created a spreadsheet detailing what was in each box so that I would know where everything was. I had a tablet containing all the box and item information, so as each item was taken off the truck, I consulted my tablet and gave direction for where to store it. After I purchased my house, Mike, again at his expense, provided a moving van and helpers to unload the storage units and move everything into my new house.

Traveling alone.

After Ron died, I had people in the house with me for the next six weeks. I never even drove my own car during that time. Someone was always there to drive me wherever I needed to go.

For many years, I had attended a yearly music conference in Jackson, Mississippi to learn new music for sharing with our church choir and musicians. Although I had already registered for the 2001 conference before Ron died, I was uncertain about attending until I received a phone call from my dear friend Beverly in Indiana. She was a pastor's wife, a very accomplished musician, and was no stranger to grief, having lost two children to death. She invited me to attend the conference and share her hotel room at her expense. I drove to Jackson from Baton Rouge and spent the week with Beverly. Because it had only been six weeks since losing Ron, I shed many tears and poured out my heartache to her during that week. I know that God arranged that time together, for her compassion added some layers of healing to my very wounded spirit. I had not been able to sleep at night after Ron's death, but God restored my ability to sleep during that conference.

One month after that conference, my sister Paula, invited me to conduct a choir clinic for their church to share some of the new music I had received in Jackson. I began to channel my energies into arranging praise and worship choruses and choir music to share with Grace UPC. The first session was very emotional for me as I stood before the choir, wishing that Ron was in the audience so I could make eye contact with him and be assured that I was doing a good job. He had always been my most loyal supporter in every choir I had directed through the years. However, I was quickly put at ease by the response of my sister and the wonderful members of Grace as I shared the information I had prepared for them. Through the years, Grace has extended other invitations asking me to conduct more music and Bible study training classes for their members. I appreciate that Grace United Pentecostal Church for loving me and letting God use them to bring healing to my broken heart.

Taxes.

Filing our yearly income taxes had always been Ron's area of responsibility. I kept records of all tax deductible items, but the process of reporting all that information on the tax forms was a huge mystery to me. Ron had purchased TurboTax software a week before he died and had begun the process of entering tax information into the computer. I went into a panic about the tax situation, not knowing how I was going to get the year 2000 income taxes filed. Again, God sent an expert to my rescue. My cousin, Dana, an accountant for a college, offered to take some vacation time and help me get my taxes filed. She told me what kind of information to gather, and then she met me in Baton Rouge and spent several days going through all my paperwork and completing my taxes. She also did my 2001 taxes. In 2002, I took a six-week H & R Block tax course to learn how to do my own taxes. Dana reviewed my 2002 taxes to make sure I had done everything correctly, and every year since then, I have done them myself.

2001 – 2005 Highlights

2001

Virginia Beach – Baton Rouge – Springfield

After leaving Iowa and putting all my things in storage in Springfield, I followed my parents to Baton Rouge and spent a short time with them. Then I flew to Virginia Beach, Virginia to spend a month with Raymond. I had a window seat and cried during most of the plane trip as I remembered the previous trip to Virginia Beach with Ron to spend Christmas with Raymond. That was the last time Raymond saw his dad alive.

My days in Virginia Beach had some structure for the first time since Ron had died. I cooked meals for Raymond and me each night and drove to the grocery store when needed. I was scheduled to teach a choir workshop at my sister's church when I returned to Baton Rouge, so we rented a small keyboard and while Raymond was at work, I spent the days preparing music for the workshop.

We took a trip to Raleigh, North Carolina one weekend during my visit. We stayed in the same motel that Ron and I had stayed in the year before when we had attended Raymond's college graduation. Bittersweet memories.

The day after our return from Raleigh would have been mine and Ron's twenty-eighth anniversary. I tried to keep from being sad, but my first anniversary without him was so lonely. I had several phone calls during the day; one of them came from a cousin who had unexpectedly lost her husband thirteen years earlier. I cried during the phone call, but was comforted because she understood exactly what I was feeling. That night I cooked hamburgers for supper, and Raymond and I spent the evening at home reminiscing about Ron.

From Virginia Beach I flew back to Baton Rouge for three days of teaching a choir workshop and visiting with my parents. All too soon, the day arrived for me to drive my car ALONE back to my new home in Springfield. I had never done anything like that in my entire forty-five years, so I had many people giving me advice about how to be safe during my first long-distance trip by myself. My mother and Aunt Rachel came up with an idea to stuff some of my dad's clothes with newspapers and

49

put a hat on it. They place the dummy in the passenger seat so it appeared that someone was with me. As I traveled that day, occasional glances to the dummy beside me made me sadder and sadder. Finally, during a stop for gas, I folded the clothes up and stuck them in the floorboard in the back seat. I arrived safely that afternoon at my in-laws' house where I was greeted by Russell and Rodney.

That first cross-country trip alone was preparation for dozens of trips in the coming years. I never liked driving more than a hundred miles at one time when Ron was alive. But God sure changed me, and now, I think nothing of getting in the car and driving 1,000 plus miles on a single trip. I typically average driving 20,000-30,000 miles a year.

Father's Day

When I awoke on the first Father's Day after Ron's death, I began crying. My husband and father of our children was not here for us to honor. I could not stop crying. My pastor told me to stay home from church and spend time with my two sons. We all got dressed and drove out to the beautiful cemetery where Ron was buried. The boys walked away and gave me some time alone. I sat on the ground next to his grave and cried until I had no more tears to cry. The boys finally walked back to the grave and helped me get to my feet. They took me to a restaurant for a late lunch, but I was still too distraught to eat.

Iowa

Part of my heart had been left in Iowa with the sweet people we had helped to pastor during our final two years. I drove back to Glenwood on three occasions during the remainder of 2001. I would fill the days with visits and lunch engagements with everyone I could possibly meet during my visit. The Poes continued holding Wednesday night services at the Bartlett church, and I would attend those services when I came into town. During one of those visits, my friend, Laura, was baptized and filled with the Holy Ghost. She was the Realtor who had sold us our house when we first moved to Glenwood. My sister, Paula, flew to Omaha and met me during one of the visits. She wanted to meet the people we had ministered to and learn more about our time in

50

Glenwood. We also spent time shopping for clothes because I had lost so much weight that nothing fit anymore. Each time I left to return home, part of my heart remained with the people who had become so precious to me. I knew though that my place was in Springfield near my children.

Christmas in Baton Rouge

My parents planned a big family get-together for Christmas 2001. All three of my boys joined me for the event. The first Christmas without Ron was yet another bittersweet experience. We all met in the fellowship hall of my sister's church. I enjoyed the food and opportunity to visit with family that I

usually saw only once or twice a year. The difficult time came when the picture-taking started. I had to leave the room when my niece asked for a picture of my siblings and their spouses. How could I smile in a picture where everyone had a husband or wife except me? I got through it by God's grace and produced a sad smile for this first solo sibling picture.

Through the years, I would feel those sad feelings for Ron when another "first" event would occur. My first birthday without him. Rodney's college graduation. The marriages of all three sons. The births of all six grandchildren. Publishing my first book. I have wished hundreds of times that he could have known about the good things that have happened in my life as I have gone on without him by my side.

2002

This second year highlights included trips to Virginia Beach, Virginia, Washington, DC, Phoenix, Arizona, and both Carolinas. A bigger highlight was a visit from my parents to my home in Springfield that summer

Raymond was still living in Viriginia Beach, so I flew out and spent several weeks with him around the time of my twenty-ninth anniversary. I got introduced to his bird "Fruitcake" who loved to sit on top of his cage, then fly off and sit on my shoulder while I was cooking; or he would follow us through the house making his funny bird noises. He loved to peck at my hair. I was always a little fearful of getting my fingers too close to that huge beak of his. I tolerated him sitting on my shoulder or in my lap, but I was always worried that he would drop a *gift* on me. We had to constantly be on the lookout for his little deposits on the floor as he wandered through the house.

During that visit, Raymond took some vacation time, and we drove to Washington, DC for a few days. My nephew, Richard, worked for Missouri Congressman Roy Blunt, and he gave us some specialized tours of the Capitol and other places in the city. My first visit to the the Holocaust Museum was a very sobering, emotional experience. Ron's brother, Mike, also joined us for a portion of the trip. We even had a professional photo shoot with Congressman Blunt. He gave us signed copies of the picture.

Congressman Roy Blunt, Raymond, Pam, Mike, Richard

Rodney and I visited the Carolinas during June to attend a wedding, and Raymond and I flew to Phoenix, Arizona in September to attend our annual church General Conference. Any time spent with my sons brings me great joy. They each have some of Ron's characteristics, and being with them brings back memories of their dad.

2003

Raymond moves to Springfield

Year three included trips to Baton Rouge and Colorado, but the big highlight of this year for me occurred when Raymond took a job in Springfield with Charles Schwab and moved there in May. Russell and I traveled to Virginia to help Raymond with the loading of his things. Then

Russell pulled a trailer back home for Raymond, who followed later in his car. Raymond stayed with me while looking for a house to purchase. Three months later, God provided a house two doors away from me. Ron and I had never lived near either of our families, so having a son as a neighbor was a dream come true. Besides, in times of need as a widow, having a son nearby would be a great help to me.

Colorado vacation

In July my Aunt Rachel and I flew to Colorado for a little vacation. She became single the same year I did, so we immediately formed a very close bond which has lasted through all these years. She was a high school counselor during much of her career, and I have leaned on her pretty heavily for counsel through the years.

My flight from Springfield to Denver was spent reading some kind of Bible-related book. A younger lady was sitting beside me, next to the window. She kept her head turned away from me during the entire trip. Just as we were getting ready to land in Denver, she spoke to me and said she had noticed I must be a Christian from the book I was reading. She went on to say that her mother was dying in a town over an hour away from Denver, and she was hoping she would arrive before she passed. Her husband and children in Texas were on their way to Colorado by car. She asked me to pray for her. I prayed a very short prayer before we got off the plane. We exchanged contact information, and I wrote her a couple of times, but I never heard from her again. I often wondered if she had made it to her mother's side in time.

We both flew in to Denver at different times for our getaway. I had reserved a rental car, and Aunt Rachel picked it up since she arrived first. Upon my arrival after 10 PM, I called her to come and get me. After getting my luggage from baggage claim, I walked outside, but she was not there. I called her, and she said she had been circling around over and over, but did not see me. I was getting a little nervous because it was so dark, and there were no people in the area where I was waiting. What we were not aware of at the time was that the Denver airport has several levels for departures and arrivals. While she was frantically searching for me on one level and saying to herself, *I've got to find her*, I was on a different level, wondering where she was. We finally figured it out and made our connection. Then we drove to our hotel in Denver for the night.

 We visited places that held significance for us during the years we had both lived in Colorado. We had lunch with my former pastor and his wife in Denver. We drove by the houses where each of us had lived in Boulder. We attended Sunday church in Boulder. The organ that Aunt Rachel

had bought and placed in the church during their years of pastoring there was still there. She was invited to play it and sing during the evening service. There was a day trip to the mountains with Sue, a high school friend who was in my wedding. Then we spent a whole day in Estes Park and Rocky Mountain National Park.

At some point during our visit, Aunt Rachel noticed some scratches on the driver's door of the rental car. We could not remember if they were there when we got the car, or if they had happened somewhere while we had it. Aunt Rachel became concerned that the rental agency would charge us for damages when we returned the car. We did a search on the computer and learned what color paint was on the car. We then made a phone call to the local dealer and were told that they had little bottles of the color we needed in stock. We drove over and bought the paint. First, we washed the area really well and applied the paint. It looked worse after we painted it than it did before. Our final solution to the dilemma was to make sure the door was real dirty when we returned the car. Fortunately, they never even looked at the car, but we sure sweated that one out until the car was returned.

Nixons Celebrate 50th Anniversary

My parents celebrated their fiftieth wedding anniversary in November, and all of my siblings and their families came to celebrate this milestone event. I honor my parents for their godly marriage and example to our family. So many marriages today end before reaching that mile marker. (At this writing, they have recently celebrated their 64th anniversary.)

My cousin's husband, Wayne, took professional pictures of all the family. Again, all this photo-taking was bittersweet since I was the only single one of my siblings in the family now that Ron was no longer by my side. Through the years, these milestone occasions in others' lives tend to leave me feeling quite sad as I remember all over again that I will never achieve milestone occasions like this one in my own life.

Volunteer Work

When I was home, I stayed busy with teaching home Bible studies and volunteering at our local jail. Another "first" for me occurred in April. I coordinated a one-day home Bible study and soul-winning seminar, and even taught several sessions in the seminar. This was the beginning of God's plan to launch me into future public speaking opportunities.

2004

Bolivia, South America trip

The highlight of year four was a trip to Bolivia, South America in March to attend the dedication of a church building that had been built in Ron's honor. A group of twelve people from our church including two of my sons, took the trip with me. The missionaries, Darrell and Cindy Collins, arranged a tour of several cities in the country during the week-long stay. This picture shows all of our group posing in a gazebo in the old town of Tarata.

Two of the days were spent in Trinidad where we attended the dedication of the church that was built in Ron's memory. Everyone who attended the service signed a guest book, and the Collins gave the book to me after the service. My brother-in-law preached the dedication message. I sang the song "I Bowed on my Knees and Cried Holy" in English and Spanish, and Rodney accompanied me on the guitar. A beautiful plaque with mine and Ron's picture on it had been made to hang in the church. After service, the young pastor asked to take a picture with my boys and me holding the plaque. He asked Darrell to tell my boys that he understood their sorrow over losing their dad because he too had lost his dad when he was young.

The city of Trinidad is known as the city of sloths and motorcycles. You could sit in the main plaza of the city and watch the sloths in the trees move v-e-r-y s-l-o-w-l-y down the trees and onto the ground. If they got near the street, people would pick them up and move them to a tree away from the street. During our two-day stay, several in our group rented motorcycles and toured the city. An accident with one of our group members involved some negotiating by Darrell as well as cash exchanges to cover the alleged damages to the motorcycle.

After the week was over, all the group returned home to Missouri, but I remained in Bolivia for an additional six weeks. I stayed with our missionary friends, Darrell and Cindy Collins. During this time, we traveled to several different cities to teach leadership seminars. There were

many emotional moments during that trip as we visited many of the same places Ron and I had visited in 1999. However, the most difficult moment in the trip occurred the day the Collins and I traveled to the city of Tarija. Not only did we stay in the same hotel that we had visited in 1999, but I was also given the SAME room where Ron and I had stayed. Memories! Memories flooded my mind that night. *Lord, why isn't he here*

56

with me? We wanted to do missions work together, and here I am in the SAME room in the country of our dreams without him. My heart was very heavy that night.

A joyful moment during that trip occurred one night as I was praying in the altar with the daughter of an English-speaking family who was in the service. The little girl received the Holy Ghost, and she gave me a big hug when she finished praying. Nothing can surpass the delight experienced when someone obeys the Gospel and is filled with the Holy Ghost.

After our leadership training tour was over, I was invited to teach four lessons on music ministry and outreach in the Bible College in Cochabamba. (I had taken a conversational Spanish class before our trip to refresh my high school and college Spanish. Darrell was my interpreter, but I occasionally attempted saying a few Spanish words from my lessons.)

Although I enjoyed the time spent in Bolivia, I decided that at this point in my life, doing associate missions work as a single woman was not for me. I needed to be close to my boys in Springfield. It was a welcome sight to me when my plane touched down in Springfield, Missouri after a seven-week absence. It was good to be home again!

Lucille

In February I attended the wedding of a niece in Baton Rouge. While I was there, I went with my parents to the Saturn dealership because they needed to have some maintenance done on their car. Just as we were getting ready to leave, a nicely dressed lady came over and spoke to me. She said I looked like a woman of prayer, and she needed some prayer. She had arthritis in her hands. I told her I would pray. We exchanged contact information, and over the next several months, we spoke on the phone several times. God keeps enlarging the geographical area of my garden as I continue to plant seeds.

 I visited Baton Rouge again in July and invited Lucille to attend church with me on Sunday. She came and God filled her with the Holy Ghost in that service. She was so ecstatic! Since that day, we have continued to communicate by phone or mail, and when I visit my parents in Baton Rouge, she often attends church with me and my parents. The fruit of my labors doesn't usually appear so quickly, but this time, I was privileged to enjoy the harvest of a new soul.

Emergency trip to Baton Rouge

A significant highlight of praise this year occurred in October. During a routine test for my dad at a cardiology clinic, something went wrong, and he went into a coma. He was rushed to the hospital, and after repeated attempts to get a response from him failed, the doctors told my mother to call in the family as they didn't expect him to live. I could not get a flight out that day, but God gave me a scripture from Isaiah 60:4 that removed all fear from my heart. It said, *"Lift up thine eyes round about, and see: all they gather themselves together, they come to thee: thy sons shall come from far, and thy daughters shall be nursed at thy side."* When I arrived the next afternoon, all of my brothers and sisters had come in from different parts of the country. As I walked into the hospital room, we all stood around the bed, just like the Bible said. Daddy was awake and had come out of the coma with no apparent harm. After several days of testing, the doctors could find no apparent cause for the lapse into the coma, nor could they understand why he came out of it. Many health problems that my dad had dealt with for years were completely gone after he woke up from the coma. The hospital staff admitted that a miracle had taken place. People kept coming into his room to see the man they all thought was going to die. He was discharged from the hospital four days after he went in. My family was so thankful for the "gift of life" that God granted to my dad. To God be all the glory!!

Caribbean Cruise

Several weeks after the scare with my dad's health, my parents and I joined Aunt Rachel and a group of over thirty people from her church for a seven-day Caribbean cruise out of Galveston, Texas. Because we had come so near to losing my dad just a few weeks before, this trip with my parents was especially meaningful to me. Aunt Rachel's friend, Mary, from California also joined us there.

The waters were very rough during most of the cruise; in fact, most of the people in our group were too nauseated to get out of their beds. Fortunately, I had cruised a couple of times before and had learned about the capability of ginger to combat nausea and soothe upset stomachs. I never got sick, but I remember seeing cabin stewards come into the rooms of those in our group and offer them sliced apples to calm their nausea.

We spent port time in Cozumel and Belize. Our missionaries in Belize, Bro. and Sis. Sawyer, met the five of us at the dock the day we arrived, and they toured us all over the city and surrounding areas. We saw the church and were able to get a closer look at real life in the country than if we had taken a cruise-provided tour.

2005

Raymond and Russell Marry

The major highlights of year five were the marriages of my two oldest sons. I experienced two more major "first" events without Ron. Raymond and Desiree had a beautiful church wedding in May. My parents and two sisters flew into Springfield to celebrate the event. My sister, Patti, baked the wedding cake, and it was not only beautiful, but also very tasty as well. Patti also cooked the delicious chicken spaghetti that was served at the rehearsal dinner. Even though it has been almost five years since losing

Ron, the "first" wedding without him brought moments of sadness to my heart. Being ushered in and out of the wedding alone made me sad. Family picture-taking afterward without him made me sad. I wish he could have

met Desiree and her family.

Russell and Ashley married in July. They opted to have a simple, private wedding in Eureka Springs, Arkansas. Ashley has been such a delightful addition to our family. I could imagine she and Ron would have enjoyed bantering back and forth. But she missed out on knowing such a great man.

General Conference and Impact DC Crusade

In September, my friend, Donna, traveled with me to Richmond, Virginia to attend our annual church General Conference. During the event, we participated in some street meetings to invite people to attend the Friday night service at the conference.

After the conference was over, we rented a car and drove to Washington, DC to participate in an Impact DC Crusade. We attended services at night and street meetings during the day at the Upper Senate Park next to the Capitol. The youth choir from Mattoon, Illinois provided the music for the daily street meetings. It was exciting to be a part of seeing a number of people filled with the Holy Ghost in those outdoor services.

During our off-time of the three-day visit, my nephew, Richard Eddings, arranged for a guide to give us a tour of the Capitol. There was one other family with three boys in our tour group who also happened to be from the Springfield area. This family had also attended the General Conference in Richmond and decided to visit Washington before going home. Richard gave us a tour of Congressman Roy Blunt's offices in the Capitol when we finished our tour. We stepped outside his office onto a balcony facing the Washington Mall with the Washington Monument in the background. We also toured the White House and saw DC by "trolley." We were able to get on and off the trolley whenever we wanted, so we visited a couple of Smithsonian Museums and the Washington Cathedral during the tour.

2006-2010 Highlights

2006

Rodney's graduation

Another one of those happy/sad occasions occurred in May when Rodney graduated from college. Happy because another son had completed his education, but sad because Ron was not there to celebrate with us. I tried to make it special for him by hosting a reception afterward with family and friends.

First grandchild

Russell and Ashley sold their home and bought acreage to build a home in the mountains south of Springfield. While they were building, I invited them to live with me. On August 4, 2006, little Kevin James Eddings came into our lives. It was love at first sight. I had taken Ashley to the hospital late in the evening. Russell had left work early to meet us there. It was a long night with no sleep for any of us. Ashley's mother, Cindy, joined us, and we played games in the labor room  while we waited. Sweet Kevin was finally born at 4:19 pm, and I was able to hold him when he was just minutes old. Holding new life in my arms added another layer of healing to the loss of my husband.

The thrill of becoming grandma for the first time was somewhat dampened by the knowledge that my grandson would never know what an amazing grandpa Ron would have been, and Ron would never know his grandchildren. I have many photo albums in my home and have tried to talk to the children about their grandpa and let them know how much he would have loved them.

Having Kevin in my home was such a delight, and I really enjoyed my new role as Grandma. I was able to observe many of the first moments in his life during the seven months the family lived with me before moving to their new home. Moments when he rolled over the first time; cut his first tooth; sat up on his own and began crawling. God granted me such a beautiful gift by letting my kids stay with me when the first grandchild was born.

Volunteer activities

There was an increase in Bible study teaching this year. Once a week found me and our team of ladies from church teaching a class at the jail. In those early years, we saw many ladies receive the Holy Ghost in our weekly classes. That year I averaged teaching ten home Bible studies each week, including a weekly class at a church that was not part of my denomination. I had received an invitation from the pastor's wife to come in and teach them about the Holy Spirit. Those classes continued for months. In time, the pastor received the Holy Ghost and began teaching the Holy Ghost message to his church.

Prayer Conference

In 2003, a shopping trip to a local thrift store put me in contact with a local prison ministry group called Praise Keepers. They would offer a place for women to stay after they returned to society from prison or the local jail and assist them in finding employment. This local group also had affiliations with groups in other states. Because of my work at Greene County jail, I began teaching Bible studies to some of the women who were enrolled in their program.

In 2004, an opportunity became available for Praise Keepers to spend a weekend ministering at the Missouri State Women's Prison in Vandalia, and I was invited to go with them. While there, I met a lady from Illinois who was part of the Praise Keepers ministry team. She was Spirit-filled, and I enjoyed conversing with her about the things of God during that weekend. God opened a door for me to share my experience of being baptized in Jesus name as a nine-year-old girl. She had never heard of baptism in that manner. She asked for more information; after I returned home, I emailed her some scriptures to study. We continued communicating on the subject of Jesus name for a couple of years.

In 2006, she told me she wanted to be rebaptized in Jesus' name. We arranged to attend a World Network of Prayer Conference in St. Louis in June. I contacted my uncle, Rev. Terry Bushnell, who contacted one of the area ministers about using his church for a baptism. We received permission to meet at a local church, and Georgia was rebaptized in the precious name of Jesus.

Wedding and Teaching

In August, I flew to Louisiana and traveled to Atlanta with my family to attend a nephew's wedding. Since I didn't visit Atlanta very often, it was a treat to attend this wedding and see my two brothers and their families along with other friends we had met in the area during the years our family lived in North Carolina.

After our return from the wedding, I taught a class on soul winning and home Bible studies to the leaders in the church pastored by my brother-in-law, Rev. Glenn Murphy. From there, I traveled to a church in Indian Village, Louisiana, pastored by my uncle, Rev. Terry Bushnell. He had invited me to teach a lesson about soul winning from personal experience to show that a person doesn't have to be a preacher to be a soul winner. I prepared a slide presentation to illustrate some of the opportunities I had experienced for witnessing, teaching Bible studies, and bringing new people to the Lord over my lifetime. Little by little, God was using my family to open doors for leading me into the new ministry of public speaking.

2007

Two Moves

Two significant changes occurred in my life this year. The first one occurred in March when Russell's family moved into their new home twenty-five miles away, taking with them my little ray of sunshine, Kevin. After having him in my home for seven months, it was quite an adjustment for him to leave. However, Russell and Ashley were very generous with him, and they allowed me to come and get him on Friday most every weekend and keep him until after church on Sunday. Then I would bring him home. Consequently, I developed a close bond with Kevin which continues to this day.

The second event occurred in September when my youngest son, Rodney, decided to move to New Jersey with a college friend. Although I had been alone many times during my marriage when Ron traveled for business, it never bothered me because I knew he would return. But the day Rodney moved to New Jersey, I experienced another "first." Now, for the first time in my life, I would be living alone. When I married, I had moved from my parents' home to Ron's home. After he died, I moved to my own home with Rodney, and now he was moving away. I experienced a period of grieving all over again. Fortunately, the grief was eased due to the fact that Raymond and Des lived nearby, and Kevin spent most every weekend with me. It really helps to have a network of supportive family or friends to help you through the challenging times.

Teaching at home and away.

Throughout this year I continued teaching the ladies in my weekly class at the county jail in addition to several home Bible studies each week. But, I added a new volunteer activity in May at the Springfield Pregnancy Care Center. I worked one afternoon a week with the nutritionist teaching the girls about proper nutrition during and after pregnancy. I usually assisted in class preparation and copying handouts for the girls. On occasion, the nutritionist couldn't be there, so I conducted the class.

In March I taught a three-day seminar in my uncle's church in Indian Village on the subjects of Altar Ministry, Soul Winning, and Teaching Home Bible Studies. Since I have quite a few family members in this church, the lessons were well received. Very slowly, God was removing my fear of public speaking and opening new doors for me to share the knowledge He had given me.

2008

Rodney Visits

Rodney returned home from New Jersey for a few days in May. We got together each day to eat, play games and enjoy family time. Twenty-one-month-old Kevin was especially happy to see Uncle Rod so they could roughhouse together. All too soon it was time for him to return to work.

Kevin Turns Two

My little blue-eyed Kevin turned two August 4. Ashley arranged to have someone make an Elmo birthday cake for him, and she hosted a party for the family. I still had the joy of keeping him on weekends. When he was home, he would often bring the phone to Ashley and say, "Talk to MawMaw, please. She would call me, and he would chatter in his special little language to his MawMaw. Sometimes he would call when I was unavailable, and he would leave a voice message. I still have ten messages on my phone from him when he was between the ages of three and seven. Even now, it brings a smile to my lips when I go back and listen to that little voice who always ended each message with, "Love you. Bye."

I realize that not every widow has family or little ones with whom to make memories. But if you can find a young child to bring into your life, those little ones can provide more healing and restoration of your joy than you can imagine.

Birthday Reunion Interrupted by a storm

In August, my mother turned seventy. My siblings planned a special reunion and celebration for her at a restaurant in Baton Rouge. My brothers and their families came from Atlanta, and I drove in from Springfield. Other family from around Louisiana came for the party. I had planned to spend extra time in the area with my parents, but unfortunately, Hurricane Gustav was in the area and had already dumped enormous amounts of rain in the southern part of Louisiana. Since no one knew how strong the storm would be when it made landfall, I decided to return home to Missouri. I spent the night with my parents and left early the next morning. The rains had caused flooding along some of the major highways and consequent detours along the way. It was a long day of traveling through heavy traffic that was trying to escape the area, but I finally arrived home safely.

General Conference in North Carolina

In October, my friend, Eva, from church accompanied me to Greensboro, North Carolina to attend our annual church General Conference. It was Eva's first visit to North Carolina, so we left a little early to allow time for sightseeing. We spent our first day in the Hendersonville/Asheville area. I drove Eva to our beautiful mountain-top home that we had built. When we stopped in the driveway, the lady of the house saw us and invited us in. She graciously walked us through the house so I could see how it looked. So many memories flooded my mind as I walked from room to room, remembering the tasks of staining wood, painting walls, hanging wallpaper, choosing flooring, light fixtures, cabinets, etc. Some flooring and light fixture changes had been made, but the house was still beautiful twenty-five years later. The lady was going through treatments for cancer.

She asked me if I was Spirit-filled, and I said yes. She told me she always believed that the builders of that house had been Spirit-filled because there was such a spirit of peace in the home. Before we left, the three of us joined hands and prayed together. What a testimony that our godly lifestyle in that home was still ministering to a cancer patient twenty-five years later. After leaving my former home, we drove through Pisgah Forest and stopped at the famous Looking Glass Falls. My family used to take all our out-of-town visitors to this falls, and I have numerous pictures in old photo albums of this place. We then drove along the Blue Ridge Parkway, enjoying the beauty of the colorful leaves on the trees. Traffic gets pretty heavy on the Parkway in October due to people coming from miles around to view the spectacular fall colors. Once we arrived in Asheville, we turned onto the interstate and drove the remaining distance to Greensboro for our week of inspirational meetings at the General Conference.

Thanksgiving

My parents arrived for a ten-day visit the end of November. They had their little black poodle named Lady with them. We all gathered at my house for a bountiful Thanksgiving feast. While peeling potatoes for our lunch that day, I found a perfect heart-shaped potato in the bag. Since that was a rare occurrence, I took a picture of it. After lunch, two-year-old Kevin entertained everyone with his performance of Kindermusik songs and rhythm patterns with sticks, bells, egg shakers, microphone, and scarves. The visit also included many games of Skipbo and a trip to Lambert's in Ozark which is my Dad's favorite restaurant in our area. He enjoys catching rolls.

2009

Music Ministry in Baton Rouge

The entire month of January was spent in Baton Rouge helping with music in my sister's church. Their piano player had just brought home her first baby and wanted to take a break from piano responsibilities for a month. So Grace Church brought me in another time to help them in their time of need. It was a blessing to me because I was able to enjoy being with my parents and my two sisters while ministering in this beautiful church.

During my entire twenty-eight years of marriage, we had lived away from both of our families, so I only saw them once or twice a year. One of the blessings God gave me as a widow was the flexibility to travel and spend more time with family than I had for many years. The bonds with my sisters became stronger as we were able to spend more time together.

Second Grandchild Arrives

The most special event of this year was the birth of my new granddaughter, Bethany Rae Eddings on April 14. Since I had raised only boys in my home, it was with great delight that I welcomed a little girl into the family. Since she lived just two houses away from me, I was able to see her frequently.

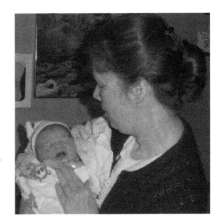

One funny memory of that year occurred one day when I was keeping her. She was playing in her walker while I was working in the kitchen. I

opened the refrigerator to take something out. In a flash, she pulled up in her walker and grabbed a bottle of catsup out of the door and took off with it. This grandma now laughs at funny little things the grands do that would have probably brought a scolding to their dads had they done something similar when they were little. It is quite amazing how I have mellowed in my older years and now have the ability to enjoy the little ones.

Volunteer Activities

I continued my weekly volunteer work at the Pregnancy Care Center and my class at the jail. But this year, I added another day of volunteer work at the jail when I was invited to help Rafael from our church with a men's Hispanic Bible Study. With the assistance of our missionary friends, Darrell and Cindy Collins, I put together a chorus book of songs in Spanish. Each week, I would lead worship in Spanish and Rafael would teach the lesson. I learned quite a bit of Spanish just by sitting in those classes and listening, but if Rafael asked me to say anything, he would give me advance notice so I could write my comments in Spanish and read them.

First Visit to New York City

In May I flew to New York City and spent two weeks with Rodney. He had moved into Brooklyn by this time. He gave me a subway pass when I arrived and taught me how to go into the city. I became quite confident at riding the subway by myself to meet Rodney in Manhattan after work. We walked miles and miles during that visit. I learned that when you go to the grocery store, you only buy as much as you can carry in your arms back to Rodney's apartment. I learned that it is no big deal to walk a mile to eat at a great pizza place. Life in that city is so different from our life in the mid-west. Rodney was a great tour guide, though, and I visited so many interesting places while I was there. Could it be that the Lord was exposing me to different places and ways of life to prepare me for future ministry?

One day my cousin, Brenda, from Long Island came to Brooklyn and got me, then brought me to her house for a tea party. We had specialty teas, scones, little muffins, and sandwiches. After breakfast, Tom, Brenda's husband, and Brenda took me to visit the beautiful Old Westbury Gardens. The rhododendrons were in full bloom. So beautiful.

On my way home from New York, I stopped off in Atlanta and spent another nine days visiting family in Atlanta and friends in North Carolina and South Carolina.

Washington and Canada Vacation

This year I was privileged to take a second real vacation. (My first one had been taken when I visited Colorado with Aunt Rachel in 2003.) Ron had been committed to taking family vacations to destinations besides visiting family during the years of our marriage. He often had air miles to fly the

entire family to places like California, Arizona and the Grand Canyon, or Colorado. Consequently, vacationing was one of the joys I had really missed after Ron died. Granted, I had done thousands of miles of traveling over the years and had taken little mini-vacations, but most of it had consisted of visiting family or attending church conferences. So this year, it was with great excitement that I accepted my mother's invitation to accompany her and daddy and Aunt Rachel to Tacoma, Washington in August for the military reunion of the U. S. Army 2nd Infantry Division for veterans of all wars. My dad had shipped out of Ft. Lewis in Tacoma when he was sent to Korea, so this was a trip he was looking forward to with great anticipation. Since none of the rest of us had visited Washington before, we decided to add several days to the trip after the reunion and tour the area. I got out maps and started doing research as we planned my first real vacation in ten years. We all flew together and rented a car when we arrived. Part of the reunion itinerary included a visit and lunch at Ft. Lewis. We witnessed a military parade honoring soldiers who were being deployed. Special recognition was given to their families. During the four-day event, I felt so honored to sit in the presence of such heroes and hear their stories. My dad even met a veteran who had been in his same regiment in Korea, and even went over on the same ship at the same time, but they didn't know each other at the time.

After the reunion, we remained in Washington another week and toured Mt. Ranier National Park. Another day we drove up the Pacific Ocean coastline and toured the Olympic National Park and Forest. We saw many huge redwoods similar to ones I had seen in the redwood forest in California many years before. The four of us tried holding hands and reaching around some of the trees, but they were too large. I was fascinated by all the huge pieces of driftwood along the beaches. Then we took a ferry to Canada and visited Butchart Gardens. I had seen many pictures of the gardens during my research for the trip, but not one picture had prepared me for the incredible beauty of that place. We took hundreds of pictures. My dad loves planting things,

and he took great delight all day in pointing out various kinds of plants and trees. After returning to the United States, we spent another three days in Seattle. Our last day of the trip was spent celebrating my mother's 71st birthday.

2010

Third Grandchild Arrives

The most special event of this year was the birth of another little blue-eyed grandson, Ryder Lee Eddings, on October 14. Even though they lived twenty-five miles away, this grandma made time to spend with the new baby and four-year-old Kevin. I became quite smitten with his little smiles and cooing noises when he would look into my eyes. Kevin was very proud of his baby brother and was a good helper for Ashley.

Traditions

My granddaughter, Bethany had her first birthday in April. Because she lives almost next door, she gets to visit Grandma almost every day. She loves to sing and color in coloring books with me. And we dare not forget the tradition of eating little Goldfish crackers while sitting on the fireplace hearth.

Second Visit to New York

In May, I flew to New York City for my second two-week visit with Rodney. We spent three days in Washington, D.C. the first weekend I was there. I love visiting all the memorials along the mall that remind us of our national heritage. We visited other tourist attractions during my remaining time in New York. We attended Phantom of the Opera one night. It was my first ever Broadway play. Another day, we toured Ellis Island and the Statue of Liberty. As usual, we walked many, many miles during those two weeks and spent hours riding subways. I also had the neat experience of visiting Brooklyn Tabernacle and hearing the choir sing. I own many of their albums and purchased two more of the choir while I was there.

Korean Veterans' Reunion

In April, my parents invited me to attend another military reunion with them in the city of San Antonio, Texas. I jumped at that opportunity because Ron had spent several months at Ft. Sam Houston in 1973 while taking his advanced military training. We had also spent our fourth anniversary there. I met my parents in Orange, Texas and drove them to San Antonio. We visited the Alamo, Ft. Sam Houston, and The Center for the Intrepid which is a Physical Rehabilitation Center for the National

Armed Forces. Our tour of that facility left me with a feeling of amazement at the marvelous advancements that have been made in fashioning limbs for those who have lost arms or legs during military service. Of course, no visit to San Antonio is complete without a boat ride on the river and a meal at one of the outdoor restaurants along the River Walk.

A second military reunion took place in Branson in November during the week of Veterans Day. Aunt Rachel joined us for that event, and the four of us stayed in Branson to participate in all the activities.

These military reunions always gave me a sense of deep appreciation for those who, like my dad and husband, gave years of their life to protect our nation and keep us free. I honor and respect those who have served.

After the reunion, my parents were able to meet Ryder for the first time, and Aunt Rachel got acquainted with all three of my grandchildren.

Editing Projects and Volunteer Work

I spent most of this year working for JEC Publishing Company helping to produce a new cookbook called "Taste of Main Street America." We found over two hundred restaurants on Main Streets in communities in all fifty states who gave us a recipe in exchange for being featured in

our cookbook. It was a lot of work, but we are very pleased with the end result. The book arrived around the first of January 2011. We had taken pre-orders for it, and had already sold about 1,000 books before we received them.

I also wrote my first book during the summer. Well, I actually was the ghost writer for a biography of a Branson entertainer. It was a fun project, but things got a little hectic with trying to do that at the same time that we were trying to complete the cookbook. I believe God gave me the ghost writing job to give me a little preview of writing my own first book four years later.

In addition to all my proofing and editing work, I still made ministering at our county jail two days a week a priority. I loved teaching the Bible to the ladies and seeing God fill them with the Holy Ghost in response to their obedience to the Word. Helping Rafael each week with leading worship in Spanish also improved my foreign language skills.

Sadly, once I started working for JEC Publishing several days a week, I had to resign my weekly commitment with the Pregnancy Care Center. Although I had built a close friendship with the nutritionist and enjoyed teaching and learning more about nutrition, it wasn't my passion. I was passionate about jail ministry and Bible studies. The editing business was in my area of giftedness, so I had to let something go to avoid being overwhelmed with too many responsibilities.

Because I have not worked a public job with the exception of the few months with JEC Publishing, people have often thought I did not have anything to do and would ask me to do busy work that was not in my area of interest, gifting, or expertise. It took me several years to learn to say *no* to requests that were not in alignment with my purpose of teaching, editing, and later, writing and public speaking. If you don't know what your gifts and strengths are, take a gifts test[5] and say no to anything that is not in alignment with God's purpose for your life.

---

[5] Discover Your God-Given Gifts by Don and Katie Fortune is my preferred resource for learning what God has gifted you to do. Ron and I taught this class in high school and college Sunday School classes in several churches we attended through the years. I have also taught it in our county jail for many years. It has helped dozens of men and women find direction and purpose for their lives.

Highlights of 2011-2017

2011

Arrival of Fourth Grandchild

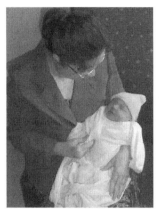

God continues to add another layer of healing to my heart every time He blesses me with a new grandchild. The most special event of this year was the birth of a new granddaughter, Kristen Jean Eddings to Raymond and Des on Easter Sunday, April 24. I kept Bethany when Kristen arrived, and a few hours later, Bethany and I went to the hospital to welcome her new sister into this world. Since Kristen and Beth lived two doors away from me, I was able to see them almost every day. It is so amazing to watch their development as they learn to roll over, sit up, clap their hands, crawl, and walk. Life is such a miracle from God.

As Kristen grew older, she, like my other grandchildren, enjoyed speeding around my kitchen and living room in her walker. However, unlike her older sister and cousins, Kristen sometimes had a passenger riding on the back of her little walker car.

Visit to New York and Boston

I flew to New York City in May for my third annual visit with Rodney. He took some vacation time and we traveled by bus to Boston for three days during my first weekend with him. Since we had no car, we walked many miles as we toured the Freedom Trail. Back in New York, we visited other tourist attractions when Rodney wasn't working. One night, we attended a Broadway play. Another day, we toured a museum and several botanical gardens. Of course, we walked many, many miles during those two weeks and spent hours riding subways. And so, the healing goes on for both of us, even all these years later. I also had the interesting experience of visiting the church founded by David Wilkerson in Times Square. We were on the go so much that I didn't do too much cooking, but I did prepare several of Rod's favorite menus during my last two days and froze them so he could eat them later.

Daddy Turns 80 and Cancer Diagnosis

My sisters planned a huge birthday celebration for my dad in September. I drove down to attend. My sister, Patti, hosted the event outdoors in her yard. I was so happy to see many out-of-town relatives that I rarely have the opportunity to see. The atmosphere of the party was one of laughter and enjoyment as family and friends visited together.

After leaving this joyous celebration, and returning to my parents' house, Mother broke the news that she had tested positive that week for breast cancer. My world suddenly turned upside-down again. My Mother?? Dreaded cancer?? Surely not!! I had only planned to visit a few days after Daddy's party, but things changed with Mother's announcement. Of course I would stay for the surgery! I cleared my schedule at home and stayed in Baton Rouge for Mother's surgery and several more weeks for her recovery. Then she began taking chemo treatments, and I had to return home. Thanks to smart phones and FaceTime, I checked in with her daily to monitor her progress and well-being. Her prognosis was good, and I continued to pray for God's healing touch.

Editing and Volunteer Work

During my years of marriage, I had learned the value of living frugally and saving. Although we used credit cards, we always paid the bill when it came due. Once I became a widow, my income was drastically reduced from what I had been used to while I was married. But my knowledge of budgeting paid off, and I had everything I needed. After meeting J.E. Cornwell in 2009, he began sending editing work my way and my freelance editing business began to grow. Through this business, God provided extra funds I needed for travel and ministry.

I continued my volunteer work at our county jail twice a week in addition to teaching home Bible studies as opportunities presented themselves. I also began homeschooling Kevin for Kindergarten in September. My life was busy and fulfilling.

2012

Time With My Mother

I started the year with a trip to Baton Rouge to be with my mother for her second chemo treatment. While I was there, we drove to visit my brother who was working at the Lighthouse Ranch for Boys in Loranger, Louisiana. He took us on a golf cart tour of the ranch and ended our visit with lunch in the ranch dining room. I returned home shortly after her second treatment.

Mother finished all her treatments in May and also took radiation treatments for several weeks. The treatments were so brutal that I often wondered if she would survive them. But Mother had strong faith in God as well as a strong will to live. She continued to get stronger each day. Our entire family was so very thankful for the gift of life God gave us after her very debilitating cancer treatments.

Broken Foot

A few days after my return from Louisiana, I fell off a step-stool while changing a light bulb, fracturing three bones and tearing a ligament in my right foot. That injury slowed me down for four months. I was in a cast for a month and a boot for three months. Then I went to physical therapy for another month. Since my right foot was broken, I couldn't drive during that time. My usually busy life of going and doing came to a screeching halt. Because I have stairs in my house, I didn't trust myself to go up and down with crutches. I had a walker in my house for one level and rolling office chairs on other levels. A huge thank you goes out to my family and several people from church who brought in food and helped me with things I needed. My daughter-in-law's mother, Cindy, spent several weeks with me. We went through the entire twelve lessons of Exploring God's Word Bible study during our time together.

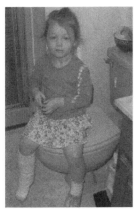

Bethany came over one day and wanted a bandage on her foot like the cast that was on Grandma's foot. I found an ace bandage in the drawer and I wrapped her right foot up. She hobbled around the rest of the day with her little ace bandage "cast" on.

I continued homeschooling Kevin and edited several projects, one of which was an 800+ page Bible commentary during the weeks I was confined to my chair. (I told the author God must have wanted him to get that project done quickly, so he slowed me down to give me time to get the editing done.) Those were the first broken bones I have ever had, and I hope they will be the last!

Molly Joins our Family

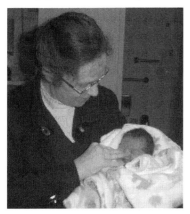

On February 9, Molly Grace Eddings, grandchild number five, was added to our family. Her parents are Russell and Ashley, and big brothers, Kevin and Ryder, were so eager to meet their new sister. She arrived with the most gorgeous full head of hair. I could already envision little bows, clips, and headbands on her little head. This new arrival caused my cup of joy to overflow. Even though my foot was in a cast, Ashley's mom, Cindy, got me into the hospital in a wheelchair so I was able to be there when Molly arrived. Oh, the thrill of holding new life in my arms once again! If only Ron could have seen these precious additions to our family. When Molly was born, Russell's family only lived a mile from me, so I had the privilege of seeing her and the boys quite often.

Molly's birth was an answer to big brother, Kevin's, sixteen-month long prayer for a sister. One day when little brother, Ryder, was two weeks old, the family was riding in the van. Suddenly Kevin said, "Mom, can we take this baby back and get a girl?" God heard a little boy's request and sixteen months later, He sent Molly. Kevin has been her protector ever since.

Chaplain Appointment

At the beginning of 2012, Rev. Cameron, the volunteer chaplain of thirty years at our county jail began having some health challenges, and a decision was made to replace him with one female chaplain and three male chaplains. Out of a volunteer pool of over one hundred people, I was selected to serve as chaplain for the female inmates and staff. I felt very honored to be asked to serve in this capacity. I was able to work alongside this kind, gentle man for several months before her resigned.

At the time I was appointed, I had been teaching weekly Bible studies there for nine years. It took a little time to meet the qualifications for this position, but once everything was approved, I was welcomed aboard. This position opened up more opportunities for me to visit inmates one-on-one in the pods, praying with them and guiding them in spiritual matters. I continued with the weekly Bible classes in English and Spanish.

Prayer Conference and Kevin

In June, five-year-old Kevin and I attended a World Network of Prayer Conference in St. Louis. There were sessions available for children simultaneous with the adult sessions. Kevin wasn't comfortable with attending the children's sessions without me, so I attended his sessions and sat on the sidelines. The greatest joy came to me on the first evening of the conference when Kevin, with tears in his eyes, recognized his need of salvation. I watched as he lifted his little hands and repented of his sins. I heard him speak in tongues as God filled him with the Holy Ghost.[6] His little face was glowing when he finished praying. With the biggest smile on his face, he told me he had received the Holy Ghost. He was eager to get back to our hotel room that evening so he could call Russell and Ashley and tell his parents the news. My heart was overflowing again. What a joy to witness the spiritual birth of my first grandchild!

Ministry in Florida

In October I flew to Florida and visited some long-time friends who pastored a church in Dunedin. They invited me to do some home Bible study training and conduct a music workshop to teach their church some new praise and worship music. I was there two weeks and taught in three services in addition to the music workshop on Saturday. Except for my ministry at the jail, this was my very first opportunity to teach in a church that was not my home church or a church pastored by family. God was gently easing me out of my comfort zone and allowing me to spread my wings and minister beyond family.

Teaching lessons does not happen without much time in preparation, study, and prayer. Fortunately, I had always loved the Bible and had committed hundreds of verses to memory through personal study and Bible quizzing throughout my life. Working in jail ministry through the years had also sharpened my knowledge because when those women asked a question, they needed an answer right then. If I had to go home and research a question, they might not be there the next week. I had committed myself to hiding scripture in my heart so I could have answers when questions were asked. The Bible teaches us to be instant in season and out of season. This readiness comes through advance preparation. From 2003 when I coordinated and taught in my first public home Bible study seminar until this first teaching opportunity outside family, God, my

---

[6] For more information on the Early Church teaching concerning speaking in tongues when a person was filled with the Holy Ghost, see Acts 2:1-4; 10:44-48; 19:1-6.

family, and my personal devotions had prepared and equipped me for this calling.

Two other special events happened during this first ministry trip to Florida. Linda Hawkins and I attended our very first Help Me Heal Conference in New Port Richey, Florida for three days. It was unlike any ladies conference I had ever attended. There were breakout sessions dealing with tough issues that women face such as abortion, sexual abuse, grief and loss, depression, stress, and family issues. God performed miraculous emotional healing and deliverance in these meetings. I left there changed. Little did I know then, that four years later, God would open a door for me to become a part of that committee and teach about my own experience of grief and healing in those conferences. Women today are under more pressure than ever, and I desire to reach those who need healing help.

The second event that occurred during that trip was a meeting with Karen, whom I had met at a church in Kissimmee in 1985 when our family was on vacation. We corresponded a time or two after our trip; then I lost contact with her. About a year before my trip to Florida, I saw Karen's name show up in an online widow's group of which I was a member. I was curious to know if she was indeed the same Karen I had met over twenty-five years before. I messaged her and discovered she was indeed my long-lost acquaintance. She even produced a Christmas card with a family picture that I had sent her the Christmas after we met. When I learned I was going to be in Florida, we made arrangements to meet for lunch one day. We met at Cracker Barrel and spent several hours talking. It seemed as though no time at all had elapsed since our first meeting twenty-seven years before. Little did I know in 1985 that God would allow mine and Karen's lives to intersect again, this time as widows. Karen has become a close friend and ministry colleague.

2013

Making Memories With Grandkids

Russell and his family bought a house in a little community west of Springfield in March. I was very sad to see them move twenty-four miles away after having them only a mile and a half from me during the previous year, but they were happy to be in a smaller community again. I continued the tradition of getting the two boys every Saturday, and taking them home after church and lunch with Grandma on Sunday. Often little Molly would cry to go to Grandma's house with her brothers, but I didn't feel I could handle all three of them until Molly got older. On those occasions when she would cry to go to Grandma's house, Ashley would FaceTime me so she could see me and talk to me. Even now, at age six, she frequently gets her Mother's iPad and does FaceTime with Grandma just to talk and show me her toys and her bedroom. I love my little Molly-girl.

On Mondays, I enjoyed keeping four-year-old Bethany and two-year-old Kristen while Des worked at church. Living so near to them permits the little girls to walk over to visit Grandma quite often. We often take walks together in the neighborhood when the weather is pleasant. Bethany also loves to bake cookies with Grandma and stir the ingredients as I put them into the bowl. I've told her she is the "best stirrer ever," so she always reminds me of that when she asks if we can bake cookies.

The girls especially enjoy coming over for "cousin time" on Saturdays when Kevin and Ryder visit. The two older ones and the two younger ones pair off for fun and games. Sometimes visits involve play time at the park or walks in the neighborhood. Most importantly, we make treasured memories.

Nostalgic Return to North Carolina

July found me driving to Atlanta to attend another nephew's wedding. I met my parents there, and after the wedding, they invited me to accompany them to Pigeon Forge for a week of touring Smoky Mountain National Park and other places of interest in Gatlinburg and the surrounding area. I am thankful that my parents have been able to travel, and I have especially treasured all the times they have invited me to travel with them. The week ended, and my parents returned home, but I stayed behind and spent several more days visiting friends in South Carolina and North Carolina. Of course, I drove by my former house again and took pictures. Since Ron and the boys and I lived in the mountains of North Carolina for fifteen years, that visit was very nostalgic and brought back so many fond memories. Memories of picnics and hiking in the mountains. Memories of volunteering in my boys' schools and leading Russell's Cub Scout group. Memories of my college years in beautiful Brevard. Oh, how I wished Ron could have been with me to take this walk down memory lane.

Volunteer Award

The twice-weekly Bible classes continued in our county jail, including leading Spanish worship choruses in our weekly Spanish Bible study class. Rafael occasionally invited me to teach a lesson in Spanish, but that required intense, time-consuming preparation and practice as I was not nearly as fluent in speaking Spanish as I was in reading and understanding the language. My chaplain responsibilities continued to present opportunities to minister and interact more closely with female inmates and staff. After ten years of volunteer work in the jail, I was presented with the Greene County Justice Center's 2013 Volunteer of the Year Award during our annual volunteer training meeting. What an honor!

Year Two Ministry in Florida

I flew to Dunedin, Florida again in October to teach and visit my long-time friends, Ray and Linda Hawkins. I also conducted another praise and worship music workshop for their musicians and singers. The sweet people at Lighthouse Pentecostal Church had given me such a royal

welcome the previous year, and it was a delight to minister to them again. On this visit, there was some free time available to take a boat ride into the Gulf of Mexico. We stopped for a short visit at a little island and picked up some seashells. We also watched several dolphins follow our boat back to the dock.

The Family Meets Jazmin

My parents drove to Springfield for a Thanksgiving visit with me and my sons and their families. They had not seen Rodney during the six years since his move to New York. It was especially memorable to have my parents here while we were all together. Rodney had brought Jazmin to introduce her to the family. She fit in with us all as though she had known us for years. The grandchildren especially got attached to her. The day after they returned to New York, I received a phone call from them announcing their engagement. Another wedding was on the horizon, and another sweet daughter would soon be added to our family.

2014

New Author Publishes Two Books

Two exciting highlights of this year have been the publication of my first two books. After editing other people's books for over twenty years, I finally got the courage to step into the author role and publish my own writing. My first book, *One Year Bible Quiz*, released on January 5. The day I held my first book in my hand marked another "first" in my life. Ron would have been so proud of me. To my complete surprise, this book sold over five hundred copies during the year. It contains one question on every chapter of the Bible (1189 questions) along with all the answers to the questions, all my teaching notes and a daily Bible reading chart for the year. It is laid out in a weekly format with questions for each week of the year. My ministry was now moving into a new dimension.

For many years, it has been my custom to start each day by reading a passage from a devotional book; then I read the entire chapter associated with the devotional scripture and often launch into more extended study and research on that topic. Over the course of the years 2012 and 2013, I began writing my own devotional thoughts from my daily studies and sharing them on my Facebook page. Due to the encouragement of many of my family members and friends, I decided to compile some of my daily devotional thoughts into a one-year devotional book for publication. That new book, *Bible Gems To Start Your Day* was released for publication on November 22. The thrill of holding my second book in my hands was just as it was with my first book.

The publication of my first book opened up several new doors for travel and promotion. I was invited to churches in several states, camp meetings, ladies meetings, a couple of home school conferences and our international church conference.

Wedding in Punta Cana, Dominican Republic

An even greater highlight than the publication of my first two books was the October wedding of my youngest son, Rodney and his wife Jazmin in Punta Cana, Dominican Republic. I was accompanied to the wedding with my son, Raymond and my parents. We planned our trip to arrive a few days before the wedding so we could enjoy the relaxed atmosphere of the resort. My parents' were planning to celebrate their sixty-first anniversary one month after the wedding. Jaz arranged to have a little cake made for them and surprised them with it during the rehearsal dinner the night before the wedding. Some of the servers for the occasion came to my parents' table and serenaded them with Spanish love songs.

The beautiful wedding was held outdoors on the beach. Rod and Jaz even asked me to speak during the ceremony. I said a few words from the most famous love story in the Bible; the story of Boaz and Ruth. Although Ron had traveled extensively out of the country for business through the years, he had never had occasion to visit the Dominican Republic. I know he would have loved the beauty of the area. How I wished he could have been by my side to see our youngest son marry and meet our new daughter.

Saying Goodbye

Thanksgiving was celebrated with our Eddings relatives on Thursday evening at the home of my in-laws. Ron's dad, James Eddings, had been ill for a prolonged period of time and was steadily declining. Almost forty members of the family came together to celebrate what we feared might be his last Thanksgiving. During that evening, he seemed almost unaware of the activity going on around him. My family took some pictures with him and Ron's mother. Before I left that evening, I leaned over to hug him and told him when he left to go home to Jesus, I wanted him to please find Ron and tell him we loved him and missed him. Although he had been non-communicative all evening, as I looked into his eyes, there seemed to be just a glimmer of recognition. He made a sound I did not understand as he raised his weak hand to me. Three days later, we received the news that James Eddings, man of God extraordinaire, had finished his earthly race and slipped into the arms of Jesus. I imagine he had quite a reunion with my husband Ron, who had left us almost fourteen years earlier. I am so grateful for the memories that were made during our final Thanksgiving visit with him.

2015

Book Number Three

My daughter-in-law, Ashley, decided to homeschool the children for the coming school year. She asked me to write a children's devotional book that Kevin could use each day to start his school day. I cleared my schedule for eight weeks that summer and put together a 180-day devotional book called *Right Steps For Kids*. It turned into a family project with the grandchildren drawing and coloring pictures to include in the book. My sons and daughters-in-law also provided input into the topics and stories that I should include. The book also included a review page at the end of each week containing activities and memory verse assignments. I decided to publish the book for other children to enjoy; it was released on October 30. Three books published in less than two years! What would Ron have said?

Bible Quizzing Tradition Passes Down To My Granddaughter

Bethany became involved in Bible Quizzing this past year at age five and memorized over one hundred scriptures in Proverbs. She participated in several tournaments during the school year and won many ribbons and several trophies. At the end of the year, she was chosen as the top beginning quizzer for the year in the state of Missouri. She is continuing the tradition started by me at age twelve and passed down to our three sons. The knowledge that my granddaughter is now hiding God's Word in her heart gives me great joy.

Another memorable event in Bethany's life occurred in October. She and the family came over to my house after church service one evening so Bethany could tell me the exciting news that she had been filled with the Holy Ghost and spoken in tongues for the very first time. This Grandma's heart was overjoyed as another grandchild was experiencing the New Birth for themselves. A few weeks later she was baptized in Jesus' name,[7] and I was there to witness that sacred moment in her life.

Traveling "Buddy"

In June, Kevin and I traveled to Louisiana for him to attend his first church camp. My parents own a mobile home on the campgrounds, so Kevin and I stayed in the mobile home with them for the week.

In August, Kevin also traveled to Louisiana with me to attend my mother's birthday celebration. All of my siblings had arranged to come, but I was busy and told her I could not make it. My pastor's wife told me that family was a priority and while I still had my mother, I needed to clear my schedule and attend her party. I cleared my schedule, and informed my siblings I would be there, but did not tell Mother I was coming. When we arrived, we parked away from the house and walked to the back door. She and Daddy were outside when we came around to the back patio. I wish I had been able to capture her expression of delight on camera as we came into view. Her joy at our coming made the long trip worthwhile.

After taking two cross-country trips with Grandma, Kevin became convinced that he needed to accompany Grandma to Louisiana any time she went.

Jaz Experiences Louisiana and New Orleans

I flew to New York the week before Thanksgiving and spent a week with Rod and Jaz. They worked during the day, and I stayed at their apartment. I was not bored because I had a huge editing assignment to complete that

---

[7] For further study concerning the Early Church method of baptism, see Acts 2:38; 8:16; 10:47-48; 19:2-5; Colossians 3:17. The disciples of John the Baptist in Acts 19 were rebaptized in Jesus' name after Paul's instruction.

week. On Thanksgiving Day, the three of us flew to Baton Rouge to spend a few days with my parents and other family. My sister hosted a delicious Thanksgiving feast in the afternoon after our arrival. Over the course of the visit, we introduced Jaz to Skipbo and Mexican Train Dominoes. One day we also visited New Orleans and introduced Jaz to New Orleans cuisine and jazz music. She met dozens of Rodney's relatives and was welcomed into our huge family. All too soon it was time to board our respective flights and head back to our homes. Jaz' first visit to Louisiana was a wonderful time of enjoyment for all of us.

2016

Panama Canal Cruise

In February, my parents treated me to a two-week Panama Canal cruise. My dad had been interested in the Panama Canal for years and wanted to visit it while he was still able to travel. We had planned to fly out of our home cities and meet in Atlanta for the flight to Los Angeles together. Unfortunately, my flight out of Springfield was delayed an hour, and when I arrived at my gate in Atlanta, the plane was still there, but they had shut the door. I had been texting my mother about our delays, and she kept asking them to wait for me. I asked the gate staff to let me on that plane, but the answer was NO! They put me on a standby list for the next flight, which I missed. After missing two more standby flights, I went to a ticket agent and told them I had had a confirmed ticket, yet they kept putting me on the bottom of the standby lists. I insisted that I needed to get out that day to get on my boat the next day. I was finally able to fly to Las Vegas and then Los Angeles, arriving late that evening. But, at least I made it, and we successfully got on the boat the next day. We departed from Los Angeles and stopped at five countries along the way, ending our trip in Miami. I read six books during that time. It was a very relaxing and enjoyable trip.

Kevin and Flooding in Louisiana

Many of my family members and friends were affected by the flooding that occurred in the Baton Rouge area in August after they received over thirty inches of rain within a short period of time. My parents were displaced for several weeks. My youngest sister and her husband also had several feet of water come into their home. The devastation was heart-breaking. My ten-year-old grandson, Kevin, was heartbroken over the losses suffered by so many of his family and friends, so he dreamed up an

 idea of putting together gift bags of school supplies and candy to deliver to children affected by the flooding. He raised donations of money and supplies, and we put together over 800 bags; then I took him to Baton Rouge in September to deliver his gifts. Two of my nephews attend a school of seven hundred first and second grade students which was flooded; they were meeting temporarily in a middle school. We brought bags to all those students and some to first graders in a school where my niece was a teacher. There were also enough bags for displaced children in three area churches. This picture is of Kevin with the school principle, a teacher, his two cousins, and all the gift bags we brought. There were lots of tears and thanks from the recipients of his gifts.

Family Moves

In May I got the news that my oldest son, Russell, and his family were relocating to Bartlesville, Oklahoma. After having those three grandchildren nearby all their lives, that was a difficult transition for me and them. Kevin wanted me to sell my house and move with them. I made several trips to Oklahoma during the remainder of that year to ease the pain of separation. I am very thankful for FaceTime that allows me to call them and see them every few days.

Kevin was able to attend his second church camp in Louisiana in June, and when I took him to Baton Rouge to deliver his gifts to the children, we also attended my dad's eighty-fifth birthday celebration. The three children also spent a whole week at my house before school started.

After having my middle son, Raymond, and his family living two doors away from me for over thirteen years, another transition occurred for me during the summer when they sold their house, and purchased another one across town, fourteen miles from me. Their move in October was a sad day for me. The little girls could no longer ride their bikes to Grandma's house or drop in with a request to bake cookies.

Ministry Opportunities

This year began with an invitation to teach a three-day Home Bible study seminar in Marion, Arkansas with my niece and her husband. Then in June, I received another invitation to conduct another three-day Home Bible study seminar in Advance, Missouri.

In the spring of this year, I was invited to join the Help Me Heal committee as the secretary/treasurer. This appointment gave me responsibility for maintaining the records and finances of the organization. After praying about it, I accepted. My first meeting as a committee member and instructor took place in upstate New York in September.

I flew to New York in September and spent an enjoyable week with my son and daughter-in-law, Rod and Jaz. They like to celebrate birthdays for a whole week, so we did something each day. One night Rodney and I rode the train and met Jaz in Manhattan after work. We ate out and enjoyed walking in one of the many Manhattan parks. One afternoon we were treated to a delicious meal prepared by Jaz' mother. They treated me to an early birthday celebration before I left. On Sunday we went to church in Long Island with my cousin, Brenda and her husband, Tom. We had lunch at a local restaurant and met back at Tom and Brenda's home for dessert. Another night Rod and Jaz took me to an Italian restaurant for a birthday dinner. On my final evening, Jaz cooked supper and set a festive table. She brought home huge cupcakes and put a candle in each one for me to blow out. After spending time with distant family, it is always hard to part and resume normal living apart from them.

My next adventure occurred the day I left their house to drive to the Help Me Heal Conference where I was scheduled to teach. Rodney had helped me reserve a rental car for the two and a half hour trip from Brooklyn. He assured me that I would have no difficulty getting out of Brooklyn and bypassing the horrendous traffic of Manhattan. That whole process may have been easy for a New Yorker, but for this Missouri girl, it was a challenge. One time, I approached a toll road with ticket booths spanning about six lanes. My GPS was yelling at me to stay left! Stay left! But the left- hand lanes were for those who had passes. I stopped and tried to back up to move to the right where the pay booths were. Then I was assailed with car horns blaring at me for holding up traffic. Once I got away from the metro area, I really enjoyed the trip. The scenery was spectacular as the leaves were just beginning to change colors. I arrived safely and checked in to my hotel. Since it was my birthday, the host church brought birthday balloons and a card to my hotel room shortly after my arrival. What a pleasant surprise!

Israel

The biggest highlight of this year was a trip to Israel in November. I had looked at pictures from others who had been going for several years and longed to experience the land of the Bible for myself. Our tour group was there for ten days, and my understanding of the Bible and history was increased significantly during that visit. Everywhere we went, we were able to read the scriptures or learn historical information about the site. The Bible came alive each day. I kept a small notebook in my purse and took volumes of notes from each site we visited. Each night, I wrote very detailed emails to my family describing the places we had visited along with the historical and scriptural significance of each place. I had a very detailed, thirteen-page typed diary of the trip when it was over along with five hundred pictures. An added bonus was the new friendships that I formed with the people in our tour group.

2017

Book Number Four

An idea for a new devotional book was presented to me on the first Sunday of this year. I told the person I was too busy to write another book, but during prayer about it, the Lord dropped ideas for the book in my mind, and I took notes. The book that I did not want to write came together in four weeks, and I had it in my hand in February. It is called *Godly Women*. The thirty devotions in the book pair a Bible woman with a modern-day woman. I selected modern-day women who had influenced my life. It sold far more in its first year than any of my other three books. Because the book came together so quickly, I immediately dedicated it to God along with all profits. The unexpected popularity of it allowed me to use the sales proceeds to pass along financial blessings to several causes that were close to my heart.

Grandchild Number Six

In April my second son, Raymond's family grew with the arrival of a sweet little girl named Sophia Elise. Even though his family lives across town now, I have tried to spend weekly time with Bethany, Kristen, and Sophia. When Sophia was several months old, I was given the privilege of keeping her one day a week while Des worked at the church. She is such a happy little girl; I call her my ray of sunshine. It had been five years since we had a baby in the family, so it has been a pleasure to embrace this new addition to our growing family. Since she has learned to crawl, she is quite curious about all of her surroundings. During her last visit with me, she found a piece of sidewalk chalk that the older children had left within reach, and of course, the chalk went right into her mouth. She learned to climb the stairs in my house when she was eight months old. My, wouldn't Ron be proud if he could have been surrounded by all these precious *grands!*

More Family Moves

In February my oldest son, Russell, was given a two-year job assignment in Mississippi. The company provided a house for the family to move there with him. After school was out, the family rented out their home in Oklahoma and moved to Mississippi. Although that move put them nine hours away from me instead of three, I still managed to travel to Mississippi three times during the year to visit them. It is hard to keep this grandma away from Kevin, Ryder, and Molly-girl. FaceTime also helps ease some of the loneliness for the children. I had the privilege of keeping all three of them for two whole weeks during the summer. They had lots of cousin time during their stay. And Grandma time ended all too soon.

In March my youngest son, Rodney, and his wife, Jaz, left Brooklyn, New York and moved to Ft. Collins, Colorado. I flew out there in September and November to visit them. I met and married Ron in Colorado, so that state holds numerous special memories. Rod and Jaz took me to Boulder one day, and we visited the church Ron's dad had started many years ago. We took pictures in front of the high school where I graduated. We drove by the house where my family had lived and I showed them the huge tree that my dad had planted in the front yard in 1971. A nostalgic drive up Boulder Canyon and pictures at Boulder Falls brought back so many memories of times Ron and I had been there. On another day, we went to Estes Park and Rocky Mountain National Park. I was able to walk down memory lane and share stories with Rod and Jaz of memories made during the years Ron and I lived there.

More Travels and Teaching

In addition to filling in as Sunday morning or Wednesday night Bible teacher at my church when needed, invitations to teach and promote my books took me to the states of Colorado, Missouri, Mississippi, Louisiana, South Carolina, and Georgia. These travels kept me away from home for one hundred days this year.

Israel Again

A second highlight of this year was a return trip to Israel in November. We were there for ten days, and I must say that I enjoyed this trip even more than my first one. Even though we visited many of the same sites we had visited the previous year, there was so much more to learn. Israel is very committed to archaeological digging and preservation of the past, so new discoveries

94

that had been made since my last visit provided a new dimension to many of the sites. My understanding of the Bible and history was increased even more significantly than the previous year. The Bible continued to come alive each day as we read scriptures pertaining to each place we visited. Again, I kept a small notebook in my purse and took volumes of notes each day. My family and friends received very detailed emails each night describing the places we had visited along with the historical and scriptural significance of each place. This time, I had a seventeen-page detailed diary of the trip when it was over along with several hundred pictures and more new friendships formed with the people in our tour group. If I had an opportunity to go back and could afford it, I would do it again.

2018

Bible Quizzing. Bethany and Kristen are now working together as a team in Bible quizzing. In a recent tournament over the book of Galatians, Bethany received recognition for achieving highest score in four matches and Kristen received recognition for achieving second highest score in the matches. While having fun traveling to different tournaments around the state, they are achieving the important goal of hiding God's Word in their hearts.

Taekwondo. Kevin, Ryder, and Molly are learning the art of self-defense, discipline, and respect for one's self and respect for others through the study of martial arts. They truly enjoy taekwondo, and they hope to one day earn their black belts with hard work and dedication!

Tokens of God's Love

God has many things to say about widows and fatherless children in His Word. Through the years, He has shown me that He loves me, and it brings Him great *joy* to provide everything that I need.

The following stories are just a small sampling of the many times God has stepped in to restore JOY to my life, including the joys I had known through Ron's love as well as the joy of living as He has met and continues to meet the needs of one of His much-loved widows named *Abigail*.

Affirmation

It is of the LORD's mercies that we are not consumed, because his compassions fail not. - They are new every morning: great is thy faithfulness. – The LORD is my portion, saith my soul; therefore will I hope in him. – The LORD is good unto them that wait for him, to the soul that seeketh him. - It is good that a man should both hope and quietly wait for the salvation of the LORD. ~ Lamentations 3:22-26

Like as a father pitieth his children, so the LORD pitieth them that fear him. - For he knoweth our frame; he remembereth that we are dust. – Psalms 103:13-14

One morning shortly after my husband died, I woke up feeling like a failure and very useless. Of course, the longer I thought these kind of thoughts, the worse I felt. Finally, the Lord got my attention and impressed me to pick up my Bible and read the page where my bookmark was. I knew my bookmark was in the book of Lamentations, and I wondered what in the world the Lord would want to say to me from that sad book. As I read through chapter three, the words from verses 22-26 jumped out at me. Because the Lord is the Creator of us all and He makes the rules, He could consume every one of us the moment we do something wrong. But His compassion for our human weakness is unfailing. If I will just repent every time I transgress His laws, He will wipe my slate clean, and I can begin every day with a fresh, clean slate. He loves me and wants to daily affirm my value to Him. Great is His faithfulness!

Giving

Every good gift and every perfect gift is from above, and cometh down from the Father of lights, with whom is no variableness, neither shadow of turning. – James 1:17

At this point in my life, I have acquired most everything that I need. The type of things needed now are gifts of time and helpers for tasks I cannot manage on my own.

God has more than adequately supplied gifts for me in the form of honest, considerate helpers. A plumber in our church takes care of plumbing needs for me and gives me a senior discount. Another self-employed man in our church has helped me with roofing and siding problems. My auto mechanics go above and beyond the call of duty to ensure that my car is in excellent mechanical order before I take a trip. My sons step in to assist when I have a need. I remember a time when the hot water heater started leaking and water came into the room where my piano was. Raymond rushed over and helped me move the piano away until we could replace the hot water heater and dry the carpet. A few days before Christmas 2017, I had a toilet overflow. It just so happened that Russell and Ashley were visiting for the holiday; the two of them worked together and changed all the toilets in my house during their visit. Thank you Jesus, for those good and perfect gifts which make my life easier.

Unselfish

Be ye therefore followers of God, as dear children; - And walk in love, as Christ also hath loved us, and hath given himself for us an offering and a sacrifice to God for a sweetsmelling savour. – Ephesians 5:1-2

God was willing to die so that sinners could be made clean from their sins and become a part of His bride, the Church. He asked us to exemplify that same kind of sacrificial love toward others.

As previously stated, six weeks after Ron died, I quit my job at the real estate office and moved to Springfield, Missouri. I had a fixed income, but it was sufficient to allow me to live without obtaining employment on a public job. Since I did not have a job to report to every day, it would have been tempting to shut myself up in my house and grieve. But a very wise pastor recognized my passion for teaching home Bible studies and soul winning, and immediately plugged me in to the home Bible study ministry of the church. Even though I was a newcomer to the area and knew no one outside of our church, I began making friends with people I met and asking them to study the Bible with me. For the first two years after Ron died, I taught from ten to fifteen Bible studies each week. These commitments gave me a reason to get up, get dressed, and think about others. In 2003, I became a volunteer at our county jail.

I enrolled in a Spanish conversation class at our local community college to brush up my skills before my next trip to Bolivia. I developed a friendship with my instructor and her husband who were members of the Springfield Federated Music Club. They invited me to attend a meeting with them one evening. I joined the club and served as an officer for several years.

As a single person living alone, it is tempting to forget about others and live our lives in a state of isolation. Since I do most of my editing work from home, it is especially easy to isolate myself from interactions with others. But when I remember His sacrifice and great love for me, I am compelled to find someone into whom I can invest time and show Christ's love.

Financial Provision

And it shall come to pass, that BEFORE they call, I will answer; and while they are yet speaking, I will hear. – Isaiah 65:24

In January of 2009 I sat down to review my budget for the month and came up several hundred dollars short of what I needed to pay all my bills. Several months before, some unexpected expenses had come up and I had taken out a loan for the expenses and was paying interest on that loan. I didn't know where to go to get extra money. I went to the church on Tuesday for my weekly prayer time. I walked around the sanctuary telling God that my back was against the wall. I just didn't have enough money to make it to the end of the month. Before I left the church, I felt the peace of God calm my fears, and I believed that everything would work out for me, even though I didn't know how.

THAT VERY DAY, when I got my mail, I pulled a settlement check out of the mailbox from one of my investments that had declared bankruptcy several years earlier. I was SHOCKED and incredibly thankful that this check had come on the very day that I had told God my back was against the wall. God already knew my need BEFORE I brought it to Him, and He had already provided the answer in advance so I would receive it on the day I asked. The check was enough to pay off the loan plus all my bills for that month and some extra for savings. **"...before they call, I will answer..."**

Since I don't have a husband to take care of little things around the house, I've learned to pray about everything. Sometimes God performs a little miracle for me, and sometimes He uses my sons or someone else to do the job for me. Sometimes I even have to pay to get the job done, but God always provides the resources I need to pay the bills. Any way He chooses to help me get my needs supplied is fine with me. I could spend hours telling about the blessings and support I've received from family and friends over the past 17+ years. I'm very thankful that in spite of the grief, loneliness, and many frustrations I have experienced as a widow over the years, I have never lost my confidence in God and my belief that He is in control of the affairs of the entire universe. Often, when I look back, I can see how He set things in motion to resolve my problems even before I knew I had a problem. **"...before they call, I will answer..."**

Protection

And call upon me in the day of trouble: I will deliver thee, and thou shalt glorify me. – Psalms 50:15

A little blind lady attended our church for several years. Because I lived near her, I picked her up and brought her home from church while she lived in the area. Around 3:30 one afternoon in October, I was driving Nona home from church. Fourteen-month-old Kevin was sleeping in his car seat in the back. Suddenly, a deer came out of the woods on my left and leaped onto my car, landing in the center of the windshield. I immediately hit my brakes and screamed, "JESUS!!" Startled, Nona asked what was wrong. I told her we had just been hit by a deer. The windshield

shattered into thousands of pieces and rained glass down in our laps. The windshield bowed in from the weight of the deer, but thankfully, God protected me and prevented the deer from coming through the glass and harming me. Since we were near Nona's house, I drove slowly until we arrived there. Her brother came out to lead her inside, but stopped in surprise when he saw my car. He invited us inside while he got a cutting tool and cut a hole in the windshield so I could see to drive it back home. He also used heavy-duty tape to tape around the opening so the glass would not shatter in my lap. I called Raymond and Des, and they came over. Kevin and I rode home with Des, and Ray drove my car.

My car was ten years old, but I had kept it well maintained. The damages amounted to the approximate cost of the value of the car. The insurance company wanted to total it, but I kept asking them to repair it instead because I knew I could not afford as nice a car as I had with the money they would give me to total it. Finally, the phone call came and I was told, due to the excellent mechanical condition of the car, they had opted to repair it instead. The body shop did such a great job on repairs that you would never have known it was wrecked. I kept the car another two years, at which time I sold it to my mechanic, who donated it to a local needy family with several children. Just ask if you want to receive.

Companionship

O God, thou art my God; early will I seek thee: my soul thirsteth for thee, my flesh longeth for thee in a dry and thirsty land, where no water is; - To see thy power and thy glory, so as I have seen thee in the sanctuary. - Because thy lovingkindness is better than life, my lips shall praise thee. - Thus will I bless thee while I live: I will lift up my hands in thy name. – Psalms 63:1-4

Each morning I make my way downstairs to my recliner in my living room to meet with Jesus, the Lover of my soul. My Bible is on the table beside my chair along with a book of daily devotions for the year. No other book can quench the thirst of my soul like the living Word of God. It is in these early moments of my day that God speaks to me. My journal is in my lap, ready to receive the directions, inspiration, or revelation that comes from reading and listening to the voice of the One who loves me so much. Sometimes when my mind gets cluttered and distractions prohibit me from tuning into the frequency of His voice, I make my way to my piano, and I begin to play and sing praises to my King. It is often in the atmosphere of music and adoration that the distractions and clutter fade away, and I enter into that holy place where He dwells. His presence surrounds me like a warm blanket, and that dryness and thirst is satisfied once again. I will continue to bless His name as long as I have breath.

Laughter

...weeping may endure for a night, but joy cometh in the morning. – Psalms 30:5

During the early days and years after Ron's death, it seemed I did more crying than laughing. In fact, it almost seemed disloyal to Ron if I laughed. But when my first grandson, Kevin, was placed in my arms on August 4, 2006, my long night of sorrow began turning to joy. That little guy brought so much healing into my heart. He spent most weekends with me during the first several years of his life. Then other grandchildren began entering my world and filling my heart with more joy and laughter. Bethany arrived in 2009, Ryder in 2010, Kristen in 2011, Molly in 2012, and Sophia in 2017. Thankfully they have lived nearby, and I have had the privilege of spending many good times with them and watching them grow. Yes, this grandma plays board games and bakes cookies with the little ones. We've traveled out-of-state to church camps and family events. There is nothing like new life to bring a smile to your lips and a spring to your steps.

Correction

Now no chastening for the present seemeth to be joyous, but grievous: nevertheless afterward it yieldeth the peaceable fruit of righteousness unto them which are exercised thereby. – Hebrews 12:11

Correction is not always pleasant, but the scripture tells us it produces the peaceable fruit of righteousness when we repent and make the necessary changes.

There was a time during our marriage that we experienced terrible hurt by a leader in a church we were attending. Ron and I were serving in several positions of leadership. It seemed no matter how hard I tried to do my jobs, my efforts were never good enough. I lived in constant fear of incurring my leader's displeasure. Many times I would cry out to God in my times of private prayer. In time, Ron and I were both removed from all areas of leadership. Eventually, God made a way for us to relocate and put that painful experience behind us. However, instead of forgiving the man and moving forward, those feelings of dislike and fear got shoved deep into my spirit. Periodically they would surface, and the dread and fear would grip me again.

About seventeen years later, the Lord brought those painful memories into my mind during my private prayer time. As I listened to the Spirit speaking words in my mind, I was strongly impressed that I needed to contact the man and ask him to forgive me. I argued with the Lord and said he needed to ask me to forgive him. Because so much time had passed, I rarely even thought about that period of my life. The Lord made me to understand that even though He had used me in various capacities through the years, I had stuffed those memories so far down into my spirit that I did not even realize how much I still disliked the man. He said now that my hidden sin of unforgiveness had been revealed, I needed to make it right.

My son and I were planning to travel to the state where this experience had happened, so I wrote a letter to the man and his wife to inform them that I would be visiting the area and would like to meet them for lunch while I was there. We set a date and met on that day. Our visit was surprisingly cordial and relaxed. An onlooker would never have detected that there had been any conflicts in our past. When lunch was over and we were walking to our cars, I finally got the courage to tell them the reason I had asked to meet with them. I said we had parted ways many years ago with a strained relationship, and because I wanted to be saved, I had come to ask them to forgive me for any hurt I had caused them. They both smiled and said all was forgiven, for they too wanted to be saved. The wife hugged me, and her husband shook my hand. You can't imagine the weight that rolled off of me when I made things right with that couple. Since then, I can remember that period of life with no dread or fear. God corrected me; I obeyed, and He gave me a clean heart.

Opportunities for Growth and Improvement

But ye are a chosen generation, a royal priesthood, an holy nation, a peculiar people; that ye should shew forth the praises of him who hath called you out of darkness into his marvellous light; - 1 Peter 2:9

Several months after Ron's death, Rev. Charles Grisham came to minister at our church. During a conversation with my pastor, the subject of his death came up. My pastor said the family couldn't make sense of his loss because he was such a peacemaker and valuable asset to the Kingdom. Bro. Grisham wisely said that God took Ron because He had something for me to do in the Kingdom that I could not fulfill with him in my life.

At the time, I did not want to hear that message. We had always worked as a team in ministry and I could not understand how I could be as effective without him as I had been with him. However, in the years since 2001, the calling of God on my life has compelled me to study and prepare like never before. As a result, God has opened doors of opportunity that I would never have considered walking through when I was married.

Jail Ministry. I had never even been in a jail when I was married, but shortly after my move to Springfield, I began teaching a Bible study to a lady who was awaiting trial for a crime she had committed. My association with her over a two-year period before she finally went to trial and prison, opened the door in 2003 for me to begin teaching weekly Bible studies to female inmates in our county jail. In 2012, an opening for a new female chaplain came available. Out of a pool of several hundred volunteers, I was selected. In order to qualify, I needed a minister's license. My pastor was in agreement with the need for the license, and he provided the forms I needed and signed them. Once I became chaplain, additional doors were opened inside the jail. Now I can enter the female pods and visit one-on-one with anyone who requests a chaplain visit. I currently work with a team of four others from three different local churches, and we teach two Bible studies each week in our jail plus weekend ministry to men and women once each quarter. Over the years since 2003, we have seen dozens receive the Holy Ghost and get baptized in Jesus' Name. Although our churches haven't seen an influx of former inmates sitting on our pews, we have continued to plant seed, and the law of sowing and reaping encourages me that in time, God will provide the harvest.

Editing. When I was in school and college, I always enjoyed English classes and had a good grasp of grammar and spelling. Because of this, people would often ask me to proofread papers for them. I even typed and formatted my mother-in-law's 700 hand-written pages of her life story into a book in 1994. But I had never dreamed of getting paid to edit other people's work. When my mother-in-law decided to get her book reprinted in 2008, I met a local publisher who invited me to begin doing freelance editing for him. Since that time, I have formed a freelance editing business and have edited hundreds of books, sermons, magazine articles, college papers, etc. for preachers and authors all over the United States.

Writing and Publishing. Although I have an eye for editing other people's work, I never dreamed of writing books of my own. When someone would suggest it to me, I would immediately say, "I don't write. I edit other people's writing." However, God had another ministry surprise waiting for me. A challenge to read the Bible from beginning to end in one year was given to my college and young married Sunday School class in 2013. That challenge resulted in me writing a question on each chapter of the Bible for my students to answer as they did their daily reading. We would then discuss them in class the following week. In January 2014, a friend helped me get those questions, answers, and teaching notes published. It was titled, *One Year Bible Quiz*. Since then, three other books have been published, and this book will be my fifth one in four years.

Public Speaking. Public speaking was not ever on my list of desired areas of ministry. I was very shy as a teenager. Even the public speaking class I was required to take in ninth grade was intimidating. During my years of marriage, Ron and I usually taught class together. I loved doing the research and putting the lessons together, but he was the one who usually presented the information flawlessly. After his death, several of my uncles began mentoring me in the area of public speaking. I knew God had called me to teach, and I had taught hundreds of home Bible studies over the years. But the idea of teaching in a church or conference was very intimidating and overwhelming.

As already mentioned earlier in my highlights of 2006 and 2007, God used my family to begin opening doors to lead me into the ministry of public speaking. Along the way, two of my uncles have encouraged me and shared ideas for improving my presentations. God has continued to change me, and open more doors for me to travel, teach, and promote the books He has inspired me to write.

Age is not a limiting factor with God. Often, we tend to think that our most productive years are between the ages of thirty to fifty. When we get past that window, it is tempting to say it is time to relinquish our ministry spots to those who are younger. But don't minimize God's ability to begin a new work in you as you grow older in knowledge, wisdom, and experience. I began my editing business at age fifty-three, and I published my first book at age fifty-eight. I continue to marvel at the new things God continues to unfold in my life.

These short stories cannot adequately express appreciation for all the people whose love and guidance has helped me walk out of the despair of losing my husband, but this I know; God loves me and has orchestrated the people and events in my life to shape me for more effective ministry in the Kingdom of God. I am His, and I desire for my life's experiences to provide healing and renewed hope that God will restore joy and provide for those who have walked the path of losing a spouse.

The Unfolding of the Call

Through the past seventeen years, God has continued to lead me into uncharted waters. Following are some of the surprises that represent my new reality.

- My editing efforts have put me in contact with ministers and people of influence all over the country. The income has given me extra funds to travel and give to needy causes.
- God is now opening doors for me to share the Bible knowledge that has been gained over a lifetime with the Church, enabling me to travel and walk the avenue of public speaking.
- Since I can only physically travel and touch a limited amount of people, the publication of my books has significantly increased the reach of my teaching.
- The proceeds from book sales have helped fund increasing ministry travels and needy causes.
- The addition of assistants to help me in the jail have eased the former pressures of having to cancel classes when I was traveling.
- As my children have moved farther from me, and my parents experience more challenges of aging, the need to travel and visit them has increased. God's provision has given me the flexibility to spend time with them as I can.

In 2001, I could not have imagined the path my calling has taken me. It gets lonely at times, and I miss Ron's companionship and spiritual covering. But I can truly say that for every token of love Ron gave me, God has exceeded each one in showing His great love and provision for His Abigail.

Every widow's calling will be specifically designed by God for the purpose He has planned for her life. Do not compare your journey with that of anyone else. You may grieve longer or less than someone else. You may marry again, or not at all. You may have more money or less money than someone else. You may be strong and healthy or weak and sickly. Trust God through the journey. He sees the end of the road and has already ordained the path that will bring Him the most glory from your life. I pray that the stories in this book have added another layer of healing and trust as you walk out of your own dark night into the glorious dawn of God's plan. Your walk will bring the Father *joy*.

Additional Abigail Stories

Dorothy Geneva Baine

Fulton, Mississippi

As of May 31, 2017, my husband, Clifton Baine, and I were married sixty-five years. As newlyweds we were invited to visit a brush arbor revival in Truman, Arkansas, and on August 6, 1952 (which was Bro. Baine's birthday), I received the wonderful gift of the Holy Ghost. Not to be outdone, the following night Bro. Baine received the Holy Ghost. We were baptized in a ditch that was overflowing with water due to heavy rains, and I remember that I was scared to death.

As time went on, Bro. Baine obeyed the call to the ministry. Our first church was in Holland, Michigan. We lived up north for many years and started several churches there. In 1976, Bro. Baine was contacted by a wood-working company in Fulton, Mississippi, and God led us south to the small town of Fulton to begin another new work for His glory.

The First United Pentecostal Church of Fulton was established in a little old white house. This house was in such disrepair that if it rained, we had to set buckets around to catch the water falling through the roof. When the house across the street came up for sale, the church bought it, and this became the new site for the church. We knew God was blessing our work when the Realtor paid tithes from the commission for sale of the house back to our church. Our little congregation grew and eventually, we added more space to the existing building to create a new sanctuary. The older part of the building became Sunday School rooms and a fellowship hall. Bro. Baine, with men of the church and other members of the community who donated their time, put many hours into the church addition and structural remodel. Children would sit on the sidelines doing their schoolwork, playing and eventually falling asleep while my husband and other dedicated men of God worked into the night. Bro Baine continued working, even though he had broken his hand through the course of labor. This was be the final church my husband pastored.

Bro. Baine was not only a great husband to me and father to our three children; he was also a great church father and leader for the Fulton congregation. But, after many ups and downs, accidents and health issues, he reluctantly decided to retire in 2003. He continued attending the church in his new role as Senior Pastor.

The newly installed pastor, Bro. Burleson always said, "If you have a problem, call me. If you want to take someone out to eat, call Bro. Baine." My husband loved to play the guitar, and he remained on the platform for every service. Even around the house, he could be found sitting in his favorite chair, playing his guitar and humming along. We used to sing together in church.

Because his health continued to decline, I always prayed that God would take Bro Baine first. I wanted to be able to take care of him until the end. I never wanted him to wonder who was going to be there for him. As his dementia worsened and life became more difficult, he always seemed to know who I was, and I know he depended on me. Then in June, 2017, just two weeks after our anniversary, he went home to be with the Lord. God answered my prayer.

I fill my days doing different things. I live alone. I'm soon to be eighty-four years old. I read my Bible. I pray. I hum a song, wishing I could hear him playing that guitar again. I miss hearing it. He could always remember how to play it and would hum along, even when he could no longer remember the words to the songs. Sometimes I know I hear music. It sounds far away, but it's so beautiful.

I also play with Baxter, his little dog who still misses him. I know because when I ask him if he misses Grandpa, he will just turn his head and look at me. He follows me everywhere and has become my constant companion since my husband went home to Jesus.

Talking to my husband's picture every morning and every night helps me. I tell him how the day is going and share news about people in the church. Sometimes it is so comforting talking to him that I forget and ask him if he wants a cup of coffee. We had such a wonderful life together. No, it isn't easy without him, but God is my constant help and friend. Things may have come against us, but nothing could steal our desire to serve God.

I have a good widow friend from our church, Sis Glenda, who talks to me almost every day. It helps to have a good friend who is near and understands what you're going through. Sometimes we go out for breakfast when the weather is good. I appreciate her. It's important to have somebody to talk to.

Don't shut yourself away. Keep going to church. Talk to people. Have a friend. Think about the good times. Talk about the good times. And always talk to God.

Donna Best

Lake Charles, Louisiana

In August 1987 my husband Bob and I moved to Brockton, Massachusetts to start a new Pentecostal church. We began meeting people and holding Bible studies in our home. On Sunday nights we would attend a nearby church in Fall River. After several months we had met several people who were regularly attending our home meetings. On Sunday evening, January 14, 1988, we took a young couple with us to attend the church service in Fall River. On the way home, we had car trouble, so Bob and our friend started walking to get help. We two ladies remained in the car. While we were waiting for them to come back a patrol car pulled up behind us. This would be one of many times that God showed me just how much He cared. Instead of the police officer coming to my side, it was a young priest. He told me later that he had come upon the accident and asked if he could be the one to give me the news. He spoke words that no one ever wants to hear. "There was an accident, and your husband is dead."

As they were walking on the shoulder of the interstate, a car with its lights off hit my husband. The driver had been drinking and never saw them. From that point on my life was changed forever. Even then I felt the arms of Jesus wrap around me and began to truly know what the Bible says about God being my husband.

A year after Bob's death I applied to a missions program in St. Croix Virgin Islands. This was such a wonderful experience for me, and God used this time to show me that He had a purpose for my life as a widow.

I have been a widow for thirty years and I can joyfully say, God has been good to me. When I started out on this journey I never realized there would be so many years by myself, but I serve a God who has given me so much abundant strength and peace through it all. I love this scripture: *And the peace of God which passeth all understanding, shall keep your hearts and minds through Christ Jesus.* - Philippians 4:7. I won't say there have not been lonely and trying times, but Jesus has been with me every day and night.

I remember a time in June, 2016 that God showed me just how He cares about every part of our lives. I had decided that for my birthday I would treat myself to a weekend in Natchez, Mississippi. It was not too far from my home in Louisiana, but it was something that I had not done in a long time. Would I even be comfortable all by myself in an unfamiliar city? When I reached Natchez and found a place to stay, I decided it was time to venture out and explore. Then the little pity party started. *Girl, what are you doing here by yourself on your birthday?* While I was waiting to cross the street, a young couple started talking to me. They were also from Louisiana and had come to Natchez to celebrate their anniversary. When I mentioned I was there to celebrate my birthday and I was alone, they invited me to join them for the afternoon. We shopped and took a carriage ride through the city. Look at what God will do in even the simple things. He made my day even more special.

Our lives may not always turn out like we thought they would, but we serve a God who will make the crooked places in our lives straight if we will trust in Him. I have made mistakes in this thirty-year journey, but Jesus has kept His hand on my life, and my love for Him has grown stronger. This scripture is one of my favorites. *For God hath not given us the spirit of fear; but of power, and of love, and of a sound mind.* 2 Timothy 1:7. There may be days when we feel like God has forgotten us, but He never has and never will. He loves each of us too much to ever do that.

Karen Brigmond

Kissimmee, Florida

The date was October 2008. The diagnosis was stage 4 head and neck cancer. Chance of survival, 5%.

My husband had been laid off work ten days earlier because of the economic environment the nation was facing.

Denial set in immediately after the diagnosis. This lasted until the reality early in the morning of June 18, 2010 when Mike took his last breath.

How was I going to face this new reality? I was immediately burdened with so many thoughts. I did not know where to begin this dreaded journey, but God had already been preparing a way for me.

Going through chemotherapy and radiation treatments, Mike just could not work, so obviously, I needed to seek employment. I came to my husband with tears in my eyes asking the question, "What skills do I have?" His answer was simple. "You have skills!"

I had always wanted to work in a gift shop, so with resume in hand, I bravely made my way to our local Cracker Barrel Old Country Store. As I entered the shop, I met the retail manager, who was very pleasant. I told him why I was there and continued in conversation, just being myself.

As we walked to the back of the room for an impromptu interview, he stated, "I think you are just what we are looking for!" After being a wife and mother most of my life, this only encouraged me to be the best I could possibly be in the area of retail. My skill, you ask? I am a people person!

The blessings of God did not end there!!! How would we survive on $7.35 an hour? This time God really stepped in, increasing our faith over and over again!

As word of our struggles got out, some of God's people from all over the country began reaching out to us, each doing what they could to help us out financially. Some gave a little; some gave a lot.

To say we were amazed by these miracles is an understatement! These blessings enabled us to concentrate on the heartbreaking medical and health obstacles we were facing.

When Mike passed away, I felt like I had lost my identity. **But *God* had a plan for me.**

In the past eight years, I have learned so much. I am doing things I never could have imagined. While married, I was co-dependent on my husband. As a widow, I have become co-dependent on God!

Trust me when I say you cannot go wrong serving Jesus. He has become my constant companion and always takes me through the times when I feel I cannot go on. He has been faithful in every way possible!

Have I changed through the years? Yes, I have. God has reinvented me and made me a new vessel to be used for His glory. I tell people all the time, I think my late husband would be proud of what and who I have become, all because of God's love and faithfulness!

For I know the thoughts that I think toward you, saith the Lord, thoughts of peace, and not evil, to give you an expected end, Jeremiah 29:11.

Linda Cook
Springfield, Missouri

My name is Linda Cook, and I have been on this journey as a widow since 1995. We were married twenty years when my husband, Larry, died of a terminal illness that he had had for over ten years. We had five children, ages 18, 16, 14, 12, and 10 at the time of his death. It is a journey I never wanted to take, but because of becoming a widow I have grown as a Christian in ways I would not have grown as a married woman. My God has been there as my protector, comforter, counselor, and my provider. The following story illustrates just one of the many ways God has taken care of me and my family since becoming a widow.

In January of 1996, I was told I had an ovarian cyst that was in danger of bursting as it had doubled in size in one month's time. My gynecologist told me if I did not have surgery immediately, when the cyst broke, I would bleed to death before I could reach the hospital. After the surgery, I was not able to return to my job as a teacher for at least eight weeks. During this time my God financially provided for my family in two ways.

The school where I was teaching allowed me to continue receiving my monthly salary until I returned to work. I had to reimburse the school for the substitute teacher, but the $ 2,500 I owed was divided by the five months left on the school calendar. My wonderful church had a special shower for my family that provided enough groceries and miscellaneous household supplies to fill up the bed of a pick-up truck and a mini-van.

God truly does provide all my needs according to his riches in glory.

Lynda Doty
Bakersfield, California

My husband, George, became sick and continued to decline for several years until he fell into a three-week coma and passed away on August 24, 2014. One month before he passed, I also lost my sweet cat, Martha, who had been with us for fourteen years.

Entry from my journal during the first Christmas alone:

"Oh it is so hard this morning. I have been so caught up with grieving for my husband that my sweet little Martha, who died only five months ago, kind of got pushed aside. She was a cat, yes, but much more than that. This morning I came across her diabetes testing kit and the tears started all over again for her. My husband and I were both mourning for her, because we had her for 14 years, and she was definitely family. She was our little girl. Oh, will this pain never end! All I know for sure these days is, Thank God for God! He's an ever-present help in time of trouble.

Tonight I am missing my Martha incredibly. It seems memories of her are everywhere, and I had a season of deep wracking sobs. This time of year is doubly hard without her and without my husband. Both were here last year, and even last Spring. Now they both are gone, and my heart is utterly broken. Martha! George! Oh how I miss you both! Maybe you are together in Heaven. Oh what a beautiful thought! I know that this too shall pass, but in the meantime, it feels like my insides are being torn out."

Present Day entry:

"And today, my King who reigns forevermore, has seen me through. Jesus has been there for me the past three and a half years!

I believe with all my heart that God allowed George's presence to be with me several times. God is like that—always knowing our needs and going out of His way to meet them. My husband is happy and at peace, and totally thrilled to be in the presence of His Jesus. He is healthy, there is no pain, he has all his toes, he can dance and skip---yes, he is happy! And he wants us to be happy. He wants us to have full lives until He comes for us too. He pops in on me at unexpected times. The last time was during the end of church service. We were all singing Alleluia, acapella. My husband loved the angels and had prayed that they would show themselves to us. God answered that prayer while he was here on earth, so I can just imagine the wonderful time he is having now among the angels! But as we were singing Alleluia that day, his presence came in so strong! He always worried about me, and he saw me there in our church, worshipping God, and he was very pleased. So was my Lord and Savior, who has never, ever failed me."

Imagene Eddings
Republic, Missouri

On December 25, 1946, James Eddings and I began our married life together. Over the years, God blessed us with five sons. James pastored churches in Missouri, Colorado, and Arkansas while we were raising our family.

In 1998, James and I sold our Arkansas farm which had been home to us for twenty-nine years. James resigned the pastorate of the church in Mountain Home, so we could move to Missouri and be near our wonderful sons, my sisters, brothers, and lots of other family. We purchased land in Billings, Missouri where we built our dream home across the field from our youngest son, Tom. We were happy to be near our children as we walked on into our senior years.

One of our sons, Larry Dean, was pastor of Harvest Ministries in Springfield, Missouri where many of our family were members there.

What greater blessing could we ask? As of now, I attend Harvest Ministries with my four sons and their families. We lost our oldest son, Ronald James, unexpectedly in 2001.

I lost my husband, James, in November 2014, just one month short of our 68th wedding anniversary. He had suffered from Alzheimer's disease for a short time before his death. I had four wonderful and caring sons to help me through this challenging transition. In time, the beautiful home James had built for us became too much for me to manage. I decided I needed to downsize. The first of many miracles occurred when we sold the home quickly after putting a "For Sale" sign in the yard. I submitted a request for an apartment near my church. The request got delayed, but in the meantime, an apartment became available near my youngest son and brother. After being married almost sixty-eight years to the one I loved, the transition to being alone was sometimes overwhelming. It was in those long, dark nights that I would again share my heart and my tears with my heavenly Father. He would wrap His arms around me and fill me with His sweet peace. The Comforter is the blessing and gift God gave us as we walk through whatever this life brings.

At eighty-eight years of age, the Lord has been and is now my comfort, guide, and caring friend as I walk on through the remainder of my life. Angels are assigned to widows indeed. I am now a member of that special group.

Anna Foster

Springfield, Missouri

Some Ways God Has Blessed Me Since I Became A Widow.

I believe God has blessed me with "travel privileges." My husband, Oscar A. Foster, passed away August 27, 1997 while we were still living in Bogalusa, Louisiana, under the pastorate of Rev. Kevin Cox. My children insisted I relocate to the Dallas, Texas area to be near family, which I did. Since that time I have been able to travel extensively.

One of my daughters, SoShawna Gray, lived in Hawaii for several years, and I was able to visit her and her family many times for extended stays. I learned to really love the people of many different cultures that make up Hawaii, not just exclusively native Hawaiians. The church they attended is pastored by Rev. Jonathan and Debbie Sanders, and I have continued to interact with the people of that congregation on a continual basis. Thanks to Facebook, I am able to stay connected with my Hawaiian friends, and that is a blessing I appreciate.

Another daughter, Michelle Jin, lives in the San Francisco area, and I have enjoyed many extended visits with her and her husband Ethan. When I am there, I attend the church pastored by Rev. Mark Morgan and his wife, Naomi, who is my niece.

I feel blessed to have made many friends with the people in the Bay Area. I have been able to help two ladies start attending that church, and they are now living for God; Ming and Keica. Ming lived across the street from my daughter, and she THOUGHT my reason for my visiting, was to help her learn English and she in turn would help me learn Chinese. That was not the reason at all! I just built up a good rapport with her and showed her love. After a period of time, a Chinese minister and his wife visited and were able to really explain God and the plan of salvation to her. She readily accepted it, was baptized in Jesus name, and received the Holy Ghost! I Corinthians 3:6-9 teaches, one may plant, someone else may water, but God gives the increase.

Later, Ming invited a group of us to her house for a "Breaking Up Idols" ceremony! She had gathered up all of her Buddha statues, individually wrapped them in bubble wrap, (to keep them from flying all over the place when smashed) and placed all of them in a cardboard box. There were several in that box! She handed the Chinese minister a hammer and told him to smash them all! We worshipped and praised God for her deliverance and victory over them, because no one had even told her to do that. God just convicted her about them, and she acted on it in the only way she knew how! Both Ming and Kieca are still serving God today!

My "travel blessings" also include Old Mexico and Israel, plus many states here in the United States. In some of these places, God has put someone in my path that I could help. In Denver, it was a deaf lady sitting on a bench at a local Walmart store. Her son pastored a church in Oregon, but she didn't go to church at all. I was able to direct her to Rev. Billy Hale's church. Hopefully, she was able to attend.

In Jerusalem, I enjoyed a long conversation with a young man checking in backpacks at the Holocaust Museum. I also met and visited with a Holocaust survivor along with her daughter who was visiting from New York. In the Golan Heights, we stayed in a huge yurt, owned by some Russian Jews, who were members of a kibbutz. They had immigrated to Israel after the Six-Day War. We enjoyed several long talks and had a great visit with them. In the Judean Desert, I made a connection at a Bedouin encampment. I am not sure we made much progress in that situation, other than to ride camels. In Tel Aviv, I was blessed with the same taxi driver which we had used for three days due to a flight delay!

As you can tell, we were not with a tour group; we were *on our own*. The trip involved my daughter, Michelle, my grandson, Joshua Royer, and myself. The trip was Joshua's graduation present, but Michelle and I enjoyed it immensely!

Here in the United States, I have been blessed to visit many states and see wonderful sights.

My older brother, Ben Pruett, lived in New York, so I've been there and have seen what New York had to offer. (It surely made me appreciate home and the Mid-West.)

My younger brother, Jerry Pruett and his lovely wife, Marilyn, have driven me all over California and some of Oregon. I have family from one end of California to the other, so I have visited there often. My sister, Sue Goodwin, lived in Idaho, so I have seen much of that state as well.

The Grand Canyon is another place I have seen; both on the ground and from an airplane. It is awesome!

Thanks to my children and my siblings for sending me to visit so many places. I also need to thank my son-in-law and wife, Ron and Sharon Knorr. He is a retired captain from Delta Airlines after flying for them many years. He has blessed me with many *buddy passes*!

My travel adventures have all been wonderful, and I thank God for each one of them. They have all opened doors for me to tell people about Jesus, whom I would NEVER have met otherwise! God has been so good to me, and I feel like these travel opportunities have been real blessings during my time of being a widow. God knows exactly how to bless each one of us, and how best to enrich our lives!

Proverbs 3:5-6 says, *Trust in the Lord with all thine heart; and lean not unto thine own understanding. In all thy ways acknowledge him, and he shall direct thy paths.* He has definitely been directing mine!

Leslie Greenbank
Republic, Missouri

But my God shall supply all your need according to His riches in glory by Christ Jesus. – Philippians 4:19.

Ed and Leslie; we were so close. Always doing the work of the Lord together. An Aquila and Priscilla ministry. We were one, put together by God's divine intervention in 1975.

We were both active and seemed fine on June 3, 2013. Ed was sixty-nine, and I was sixty-six. That day he had a job to do. I stood at the door going out to the garage and watched him as he backed out, and the large garage door came down after his exit. I realized later it was like the "last curtain call." It was the last time I saw my husband alive.

About mid-morning the call came. Ed had experienced a heart attack and did not make it. He died instantly. That very moment after hearing those words, I felt God's strength come into me. He bound me up, enfolded me, and held me. I lifted my hands to Him and said out loud, "In everything I give you thanks." His presence was so real, so there! I also heard that inner voice speak as it spoke to me, saying, "You will be going on alone now." Those words were hard to hear. What do I do now? Decisions! So many decisions! Jesus, hold my hand.

Just six months before this day, Ed and I had taken James and Imagene Eddings for a ride since they no longer owned a car. He wanted to visit the little country cemetery where many of his family were buried. We walked around that day, and as we were leaving, James turned to Ed and said, "If you ever have a need…" Ed and I both knew what he meant. We looked at each other with the look that said, *"We don't think we'll need this for a very long time."* Ed's family had longevity into their high 80s and 90s. I expected to have my husband for a long time yet. We had prayed that we could go together when the time came, knowing how hard it would be for either of us to be without the other. However, it was not to be.

Right away I called Imagene and told her, "We have a need." She and her brother came that day and drove me out to the cemetery. She helped me choose the right plot and gave it to me. Ed is now buried in that beautiful country cemetery that we had visited just six months earlier. Such a peaceful resting place!

Our daughter and son-in-law were renting a house from a Mennonite man who also knew Ed. He was a farmer, but also built coffins on the side. Our daughter called him that day, and he just happened to have a newly finished coffin that would be perfect for Ed. It was beautiful and just right, waiting there for us.

I needed to write the obituary. How should I word it? A brother and sister in the church in Oklahoma were in that business. They said they would write it and put it in the newspaper for me.

There was a funeral to plan. Our pastor and his wife took care of it by preparing the church, the music, and the dinner. Everything was done so beautifully.

How thankful I am for the unfolding of the rose when I needed it, all done by the hand of the Lord.

I am now called a widow; a name I never wanted to have. Before Ed died, if the thought ever came to mind that I'd be a widow without my husband, I would immediately push it out. It was too painful to even consider. When it actually did happen, Jesus was there. He carried me.

As I write this now through tear-filled eyes, I can say with assurance, "Oh how He cares for widows and protects them." I'm so thankful to know that as I go on alone, I am never alone. Jesus is there!

Laura Hellbusch

Glenwood, Iowa

The date was June 7, 2004. I had been at work and had taken our grandson to a summer Bible school in town. I got the mail from the box as I always did and went to the living room to sort the important from the trash. As I entered the room, I saw Charlie lying on the floor. It was a warm day, and I thought he had just come in to cool down. As I passed him, I thought to myself, *he doesn't look right*. Not thinking much about it, I sat down and started to go through the mail. I looked at him again and thought, *he's not snoring; he always snores.* I went to his side, and he was cold. I went into auto pilot, first calling 911 and then my church families.

God had been preparing me for this long before his death. When I was a Real Estate Agent, I had sold a house to Ron and Pam Eddings. Pam and I had become good friends. I had fallen away from the Lord, and Pam brought me back, reigniting my love for Jesus. I was attending church with the Eddings and had made several friends there. By this time, however, Ron had passed, and Pam had moved. I called another family who were good friends. They dropped what they were doing and came straight to my home. They showed God's love in everything they did for me. God is so good to me that He had even placed me in a medical office with two wonderful born-again Christian ladies. The Bible school I had taken our grandson to was at the church where one of my co-worker's husband was Pastor. So, I had two church families to draw strength from.

Once the funeral was over and things were a little settled, I went back to work. The range of emotions I was going through was like riding an awful roller coaster, and I wanted to get off. One day at work, I said I was furious with God for taking Charlie. One of my co-workers said, "Aren't you glad that no matter how mad you are at Him, God always loves you?" I really needed the reminder at that time.

During the first two years I learned to lean on Jesus and His love instead of Charlie. It's now second nature to lean on Jesus' strength. God has taught me I can do *all things through Him who strengthens me*. Over the years, God has taken me through a lot of hard times and has enriched my life with wonderful joys. He has even put me in the position several times to help other widows during their hardest first year of grief.

Virginia Kloster
Keokuk, Iowa

My husband, Alex, and I lived in Keokuk, Iowa for many years. He pastored the church we attended. We have three grown children: Alex III, Jennifer, and Krista.

Jennifer and Jamie married October 1996. Alex and Charlene married in December 1996. Krista was in her second year of college in 1998.

We had been pastoring for twenty-six years when on November 15, 1998, Alex's hip snapped at church, and he fell to the vestibule floor. While repairing his hip, an orthopedic surgeon failed to notice a tumor on his kidney. By April, 1999, he was not getting better, so additional testing was done. He was diagnosed with renal cell cancer and given a prognosis of eighteen months to live. We were in shock!!

At this time, we owned and operated a janitorial service, cleaning commercially. We also owned several properties.

Alex was a great steward with our finances; all the properties were completely paid for. The janitorial service finances were ongoing as far as expenses and income. God provided assistance with the business, as Krista attended college close by and helped me. Our son, Alex III, felt God wanted him to move back to Keokuk in 1997. His move allowed him to be near and available to help with the business or problems at home. He took care of the church when we were out of town for cancer treatments. I had never taken care of our finances at home or for the business before Alex got sick. God knew I needed some of my children nearby.

My husband, Alex, passed away June 11, 2000 at the age of fifty-two and a half. We would have been married 32 years that September. After Alex passed, our daughter, Jennifer, came to Keokuk with our first grandchild, Kaitlin; she stayed with me and Krista for eight months while her husband was deployed to Bosnia. It was a great comfort to have a new six-month-old grandbaby living with us so soon after losing Alex.

Alex had no idea he would die so young, but with God's help, he had wisely paid for all properties and established a business that I could use for income.

Alex III, Charlene, and family currently pastor our church in Keokuk, Iowa. Jennifer, Jamie and their family are active in Pastor Stan Gleason's church in Kansas City, Missouri, and Krista, David, and Elle are active in Pastor Shawn Meek's church in Prattville, Alabama.

Today, almost eighteen years later, I am still operating the Janitorial Service. (It is much smaller now, for which I'm thankful.) God has given me great health. God has provided for me in the challenge of being widowed with all aspects of my life. He has given me hope, comfort, help with finances and help with losing the love of my life. I am thankful that God has been faithful in keeping me and our children.

Linda Midey
Lufkin, Texas

In 2015, I walked in my door after work and found my precious husband had passed away in my absence. My whole world turned upside down in one instant. For weeks I was numb with the most devastating pain I had ever felt. With that pain came the nagging fear of how I would survive without him. Since that day, I can truly say I have seen my Lord provide so many times when I did not know where to find help.

Twice God has put me on a precious lady's heart to send money in the mail. Tears fell on those letters. She had no idea how desperate my situation was in those times. There have been so many other occasions when God came through for me. One time a complete stranger tapped me on the shoulder at a ladies' fellowship meeting and handed me $300. God had spoken to her heart to give to me. Another time a man of God slipped some money under my hand as I was kneeling in prayer. I was unable to pay my rent that month, but God saw my need. I could tell many stories about the Lord's faithfulness to meet my every need.

Not only has God met my financial needs, but He has also met my emotional needs as well. In the wee hours of the morning when I awake and the emptiness threatens to overwhelm me, I only have to speak His name, and I feel that peace that only He can give. There have been times when it felt like a warm blanket was wrapped around me. Not one tear is ever hidden from my Lord. There have been times He has healed me when I called on His name in the middle of the night because I felt so alone and afraid. He said, "I will never leave you nor forsake you," and He never has. At times He is silent and I feel He is not listening, but I know He is there, and He has a plan for my life. God has taken all the broken pieces and is slowly putting them back together again. Isaiah 54:5 says, "…thy maker is thy husband." More than that, He is my everything!

125

Cindy Moore

Fulton, Mississippi

It was June of 1972 when we were married. I was eighteen. Bob had not been in church all of his life. As it turned out, he became a Christian simply because of his intense desire to marry me. I had told him I could not marry him if he was not a born-again believer. After we were married, he attended church a couple of times, and then it was over.

My marriage was not made in Heaven. There was alcohol and substance abuse. Not being a strong person, I allowed him to drag me to parties and places I would never have gone on my own. I endured physical abuse, verbal abuse, and infidelity. After years of struggle, in and out of church myself, trying to make my marriage work in every way I could imagine, I finally turned it "All" over to God. My children and I began attending church regularly and remained faithful. My husband was put into the hands of God Almighty.

Things finally came to a head one Sunday morning while the children and I were at church. During the service, Bob came through the back door and demanded the usher to come and get me. I slipped out of service and met him on the church lawn. Bob said he would not compete with the church for me any longer and I had better choose whether I wanted him or the church. I begged him not to talk that way, for surely he did not realize the gravity of what he was saying. He insisted that he understood exactly what he was saying, and he demanded my answer. I fearfully and quietly replied to him, "God is indeed first in my life, my family is second, and everyone else and myself are last."

"Okay then," he responded gruffly. "You have chosen. But, you are still my wife for the time being, and I expect you to serve me as such. I have just gotten home from a long run, (he was a truck driver) and I expect you to come home now and fix my lunch."

With a calmness that hid the trembling inside me, I said to him, "I hope you are not the one who has chosen." I told him I would be home shortly. I left the church after making arrangements for my children to be brought home.

Life went on as it always had for a few weeks. We had planned a small vacation for the kids. My eight-year-old son, Andre, was the most excited about it. My two daughters, thirteen-year-old Tiffany and eleven-year-old Kristy, were not so enthralled with the vacation idea, knowing how volatile their father was.

Shortly before time for our trip, Bob called me from a pay phone. "Coming home and trying to get there," was his message. When I asked him what he meant, he said his arm was acting up and he could barely shift the gears on the truck. He wanted me to make him a doctor appointment. He did not want to go on vacation with his arm hurting so badly.

That doctor appointment was made along with many more after that. Bob's severe arm pain was due to a cancerous tumor on his lung. It was pressing on nerves and preventing proper functioning of his arm. His doctors, estimating the cancer to be only a few weeks old, were confident he could be cured.

Weeks turned into months of doctor appointments, chemotherapy, radiation treatment, and periodic hospitalizations. He worked when he could; his understanding employer gave him shorter runs. However, he eventually became bedridden as the cancer continued to grow in spite of medical efforts.

Church people would visit. The pastor of our small Pentecostal Church came and prayed for him whenever he asked. I was privileged to see him repent again. Before his death, he called to me one day and wanted me to look at the beautiful river as he pointed to the wall. He insisted that I should listen to the beautiful music, more beautiful than anything he had ever heard. I believe God allowed me to witness this incident so I could convey it to the children, especially the girls, who indeed asked later if I thought their father had made it into Heaven.

Ten months after the cancer diagnosis, Bob succumbed to death, at thirty-eight years old. When I left his room, I was alone. Sitting down by myself, I began to reflect and remember the events of the previous months. I remembered his tears when we were told about the cancer and the pleading look in his eyes as I assured him I would be there. I remembered his occasional angry outbursts, screaming at me that God was doing me a favor. I remembered his thankfulness for all the prayers and his apologies to me for having been so mean and ugly during our fourteen years of marriage. I remembered his bravery as he told me how he wanted his memorial service to be simple and short for the sake of the children. I remembered how he cried one day when he realized he had never taken his son fishing and knew he would never have that opportunity.

Not knowing what to feel, I began to numbly take care of business. Phone calls. Arrangements. When to have the service? What to say to people? What to do? When to stop and feel? Afraid to stop and feel.

Breaking down alone about a month after his death, I prayed earnestly for God to just please help me. Guilt overwhelmed me for the times I had felt anger. I wondered if I had prayed enough for him. I had indeed, forgiven him. I truly had. Passing judgment was certainly not my place. Perfection was not something I had achieved. Despair was definitely a familiar feeling right now. I had stayed faithful to him to the end. But, what now? I was a thirty-six-year old widow with three children. What now?

It took time, but God helped me in ways I can't explain. God became my soulmate. I became involved with things at church, truly enjoying everything. My needs were met as God became my provider. I learned to trust God in ways I had not trusted Him previously because I was so consumed with anxiety and fear. For the first time in many years, I learned to allow God to surround me with the "peace that passes all understanding." I learned to let God sustain me in all my ways.

Betty Parkey

Poplar Bluff, Missouri

I am so very thankful for the numerous and various ways that God brought comfort to me after losing my husband, W.C. Parkey, on August 8, 2011. I was surrounded with the loving support of my children, Beth Dillon, Barbara Braswell, Bill and Bryan Parkey along with their precious families. My Cornerstone Church family was such a blessing.

Although family and friends were so very comforting and helpful, I found my greatest comfort as I poured my heart out to God in prayer at home or church, reading His Word and being in His Presence. Many scriptures blessed me, but Jeremiah 29:11 was one I referred to often as I searched for my "new" identity, *"For I know the thoughts that I think toward you, saith the Lord, thoughts of peace, and not of evil, to give you an expected end."*

I attended one GriefShare[8] session and found their reading material helpful, along with the emails of encouragement sent to me each day for several months.

Women of Worth[9] Director, Sis. Jean Carney, reached out to me along with Sis. Linda Grohman, Missouri Director of WOW.

In October of 2011, I attended United Pentecostal Church International General Conference. Feeling very sorrowful at the close of the Memorial service for my husband and other ministers, I was introduced to Pastor Ron Libby, who was serving as Committee Chairman of Points of Refuge,

---

[8] GriefShare is a grief recovery support group where you can find help and healing for the hurt of losing a loved one.

[9] Women of Worth – WOW is an arm of UPCI Ladies Ministries for ministers' widows.

a ministry of the UPCI to ministers and their families. He spoke words of comfort and after I returned home, he contacted me by phone for a few months to share the Word of God and pray for me. This helped me through some very dark, depressing days as the raw reality of the death of my husband really began to sink in, especially after I had been to General Conference without him and then returned back home to an empty house.

In February 2012, I read the book, One Thousand Gifts, written by Ann Voskamp, which emphasized being grateful. Ann presented a challenge to live fully right where you are. I decided to focus on what I had instead of what I had lost and started recording each day things I was grateful for until I reached one thousand. This was very therapeutic, and today it is still a reminder to be grateful at all times. Another project that was helpful was one I took on myself. I chose to share the Word of God every day for a year either by a card, email, Facebook, or in person. This brought comfort because as I gave out, God gave back to me, pressed down, shaken together and running over.

Kathy Roat

Cannelton, West Virginia

A year before Paul *Punkin* passed, I was laid off after 20 years in banking. God had answered my prayer to be home and take care of him during that last year. After he passed on February 6, 2014 with bone marrow cancer, God blessed me with a job as a Financial Navigator for a Cancer Center. He placed me where I could help other cancer patients and their families with their journey.

There are not enough words or time to tell of the spiritual and financial blessings that have overtaken me when I needed strength for the journey, comfort in the tear-filled midnight hours, money to pay bills or pay for work that needed done on the house, or even repairs for my car.

My mother said it best with her statement, "When you become a widow, you have fulfilled that final vow of your marriage vows, 'till death do us part.'"

Sara Lemonds Sanders

Porterdale, Georgia

April 1958 was our wedding day. Six days later we went to work in the ministry. Little did we know how far our Lord and Savior would take us. We had both become licensed ministers. We stayed booked with revivals, camp meetings, ladies' conferences, prison work, church dedications, funerals, evangelism, and pastored four different churches. When God is really blessing and moving, it is easy to forget it will not last forever.

I had gone to church alone that morning of November 28, 1999 because Guy was not feeling well. He wanted me to go without him, so I did. I came home to find him lying on the floor. A blood clot had hit his heart, and he was gone. After almost forty-two years of marriage, what was I going to do? I felt like my world had ended.

Almost four hundred people attended the funeral. Our pastor and home church were behind me. It was not going to be easy. Three months later the Lord began speaking to me. *Your husband's life has stopped, but your ministry did not.*

My life changed at fifty-eight years old. What indeed was I going to do? It would be two years before I could draw a widow's pension, and I would only receive half of my husband's retirement, $112.50 a month. But God stepped in. On the way to minister at a family conference one evening, a deer jumped from a bank and totaled my car. God provided me with a much newer car, completely paid for. Someone else paid my electric bills. Food was brought to my door. God never failed to meet my needs.

After fasting, praying, and seeking God with my church behind me, I took all of the names and phone numbers that different pastors had given me and went to my desk. Praying, I asked the Lord which one I should call first. He let me know, and I began booking revivals and meetings.

No, it has not been easy. God will never let us down if we put Him first. I have been in the ministry now for sixty years with God's help. Sisters, you can do it. God's work must go on.

Pam Slaydon
Elmer, Louisiana

In September 2011, my husband, Gary, was diagnosed with multiple myeloma. We were blessed with five more years with him before he passed on January 30, 2016 at MD Anderson in Houston, Texas. During his illness, Gary determined to make the most of the time he had been given by making many wonderful memories with his family and friends. His passing was filled with grief, but we also had peace, knowing his was a life well-lived and his salvation was assured.

After his passing, God proved faithful in my time of need. We owned a one-hundred acre horse ranch that had been gifted to us by a dear family friend in 1995. From the moment we moved in, my husband was determined to use it as a blessing to others. For years it was a restful and peaceful haven to many tired, hurting souls. We have been able to host weddings for precious young couples in our church and be a place for churches, youth groups, and local school groups to gather for a fun time of fellowship, food, and hay rides. I loved our home and couldn't imagine living anywhere else, but the task of keeping up the property and the decisions to be made were overwhelming. I am blessed to have my two daughters, sons-in-law and their children nearby. Both of my daughters homeschool their children, which allows my grandchildren to visit my home on a daily basis. They have worked beside me to help maintain the property. We also were blessed with dear friends (confidantes and trusted friends of Gary's) who stepped in to help me make wise decisions regarding our livestock and help us with the upkeep of the ranch and equipment. Each time a need has arisen, God has provided. I have been able to continue using my home as a place of refuge, encouragement and peace and I am thankful that my days have been filled with neighbors, friends and family who have encouraged and loved me through the loss of my husband.

Linda Underdown
Cincinnati, Ohio

Even though my husband, Ray, battled cancer for two years and six months, I was not prepared for his death on July 30, 2008. Neither one of us would accept the fact that he was terminal. We held on to the belief he would be healed in this life. We continually prayed and fasted to see him healed.

After he passed away, I kept asking God if there was more I should have done. Should I have prayed or fasted more? I struggled to make sense of his death. During my darkest depth of grief, I knew my pastor and church family were praying for me. I knew I was not alone. But I still struggled.

Then one day, a sermon by a young preacher finally opened my eyes and freed me from the burden I had carried for a couple of years after Ray's death. I John 5:14 – *And this is the confidence that we have in him, that, if we ask any thing ACCORDING TO HIS WILL he heareth us…* (Emphasis is mine.) God had other plans for Ray. We just could not or would not see it.

When we yield to God's will, life is so much easier. There is no struggle, no doubt, no fear. My faith has grown stronger, knowing God is in control. All we have to do is lay everything at His feet. It will get better because God is with us, and our reward is waiting in Heaven.

Appendix

Does Grief Have a Physical Effect on our Body?

By: Leslie Greenbank

It is well with my soul! Yes, when holding onto Jesus for our comfort, guidance, and support, we can truly say, "It is well with my soul." We are made up of body, soul, and spirit. Indeed, our physical body responds to a great loss.

When my husband, Ed, died, I immediately had no appetite, none at all. This went on for quite a while. I would liken it to your body going into a type of shock; it has no response to food. The main symptom of shock is decreased blood pressure, and loss of appetite causes decreased blood pressure. It is common for extreme grief to cause a loss of appetite because the survivor no longer finds pleasure in food or eating.

Pam experienced this as I did, and she lost thirty pounds in several weeks. It is real. Maybe your body is telling you it cannot handle food right now. Additionally, eating is often something the bereaved enjoyed as a result of spending time with their deceased one at the table. Therefore, the thought of never having this experience again is so disturbing that the one left behind has no desire to eat. The survivor feels it is better not to eat than to eat alone. Be patient. It has been four and a half years since losing Ed, and my appetite has finally returned in full force! Just give yourself time.

I was accustomed to having two cups of coffee every morning. From that day until many months later, I could not drink any. I cannot explain that; I just couldn't handle it. Then one day, I tried drinking one cup. I was able to enjoy it, but I have never gotten back to drinking two cups. Possibly it is the same association factor as eating alone.

Does becoming a widow and missing your husband have an effect on your body? Yes, it does. The first year and a half after Ed went home to be with the Lord, I visited urgent care four times. First, it was a bout with bronchitis. Next, my back went out, and I spent a great deal of time in bed suffering great pain. I had never experienced back problems like this before. The third time, I noticed red streaks going up my breast and was diagnosed with mastitis. Mastitis?? That was a new one for me. I thought only nursing mothers were prone to get that.

While talking with the doctor, I told her this was my third time in urgent care since losing my husband. She replied, "Your immune system has been compromised." She went on to explain that grief can have a serious effect on our immune system. This is attributed to the fact that grief can actually cause a decrease in the white cell production in the body, and those white cells are needed to fight off disease and infection.

We are all different and will experience the effects of grief and loss in different ways. God will give you grace to get through this and you also need to give yourself grace and patience during the grieving process to become well again.

I hope this will help you to know it can be "well with your soul" even if you have encountered negative physical manifestations. You have experienced a great loss, deep grief, and a dramatic change in your life. There are so many adjustments to make. There are so many responsibilities that used to be handled by two, but remember you are not alone. Take courage during this time. Jesus is with you through this valley of death. It is a journey, and He goes with you.

Another area that can be problematic physically involves doing all the maintenance jobs that the husband once did. Women are indeed the weaker vessels. I've tried to tackle these jobs myself because I don't want to be bothersome to others. In fact, it is hard for me to ask for help. I have been successful many times, but I have also hurt myself several times.

Once while trimming bushes, a branch hit me directly in the eye, causing severe pain. Another time I fractured a bone in my foot while shoveling. On yet another occasion, I was trying to hammer some nails into a trellis. There was a hidden screw behind the trellis that I could not see. As I hit the nail with the hammer, that huge screw on the backside of the trellis dug into my wrist and punctured a main vein. When I pulled my arm back, the vein, still attached to the screw, came out of my wrist. When I pulled the screw out, a fountain of blood began spurting out of the vein. It was a holiday weekend, and none of my neighbors were home. I immediately called out, "Jesus!" Instantly, the bleeding stopped. I grabbed a towel to wipe the blood that was everywhere, but by the time I got inside the house, the vein had gone back into my wrist, and the hole closed up. There is power in the name of Jesus.

The fourth maintenance injury required a fourth visit to urgent care. I was washing the wood frame on my back door when a small sliver of the wood splintered off and lodged deeply underneath my fingernail. Try as hard as I might, I could not remove the splinter. When the doctor saw me in urgent care, she could not remove it either. She told me it appeared that my fingernail would have to be surgically removed in order to remove the splinter. She began giving me shot after shot to numb the pain as she probed deeper and deeper to get to the splinter. Finally, she successfully removed it. She gave me an additional tetanus shot and said I could go home. She left the room, and as I stood up to go, I suddenly felt lightheaded and couldn't catch my breath. The nurse came back into the room, and when I said I couldn't breathe, she had me lie back down. She remained in the room with me until I felt better. Later, in describing the experience to a friend, she said it sounded like I had experienced anaphylactic shock which is a serious allergic reaction to something. Because I rarely take any medications, I suspect my body had experienced an allergic reaction to all the shots the doctor had given me as she was trying to remove the splinter.

These were all tasks that my husband would have easily accomplished as the man of the house. Sometimes we do need help from others, especially the body of Christ.

Take heart and lean heavily on Jesus during these times of transition because His Word clearly assures us that He cares for widows! By His grace, restoration will come for your body, soul, and spirit, and you can be used greatly for Him on the road ahead.

Promises to Widows from God's Word

By: Pam Eddings & Cindy Moore

The Promises of God to the widow fall into three basic categories.

God's Responsibility

*A father of the fatherless, and a **judge** of the widows, is God in his holy habitation.*
- Psalms 68:5

Judgment on those who mistreat widows. God will see justice done on behalf of widows. Several translations replace the word, judge, with *defender*. A defender will guard you and protect you. There are actually seventy-eight references to widows in God's Word. If He cared to mention the widow that often, then He is certainly concerned about the care and regard for widows and their children.

*Now when he came nigh to the gate of the city, behold, there was a dead man carried out, the only son of his mother, and she was a widow: and much people of the city was with her. - And when the Lord saw her, he had **compassion** on her, and said unto her, Weep not. – Luke 7:12-13*

Compassion. When Jesus saw the funeral procession of a widow's only son, He realized that she had no one to provide for her. His compassion compelled Him to raise the son back to life so he could provide for his mother's daily needs.

Others' Responsibility

*At the end of three years thou shalt bring forth all the **tithe** of thine increase the same year, and shalt lay it up within thy gates: - And the Levite, (because he hath no part nor inheritance with thee,) and the stranger, and the fatherless, and the widow, which are within thy gates, shall come, and shall eat and be satisfied; that the Lord thy God may bless thee in all the work of thine hand which thou doest. -* Deuteronomy 14:29

Provide for them. Often widows have financial needs that could easily be met by others in the body of Christ. Sometimes they need money. The Levites were instructed to share the tithes with needy widows and their children.

Sometimes they need food. Deuteronomy 24 commanded the Israelites to share their excess harvest with the widows and their children. Often we have pantries loaded with food while widows are measuring portions of their meager resources to make them last until more income is available.

Sometimes widows need help with maintenance of their car or items in their home. Part of providing for them could involve person in the body volunteering to do these tasks at no charge, so the widow could allocate her funds for bills and other necessary living expenses. One widowed friend of mine has no family nearby to help her, so she has to pay a handyman $30 per hour to take care of maintenance tasks she cannot physically do.

The Scribes and Pharisees were condemned as hypocrites in Matthew 23 for not taking care of the widows. In Acts 6, men were appointed to look after the business of the widows' care. These scriptures demonstrate how strongly God cares about the welfare of the widow.

In many cultures, the fatherless (orphans) and the widows are typically the most destitute and often fall into the societal cracks of poverty. But God has always cared about their welfare. Because of their situation, they have learned to trust God in ways that some cannot even imagine. Help them in their times of need.

Pure religion and undefiled before God and the Father is this, To visit the fatherless and widows in their affliction, and to keep himself unspotted from the world. - James 1:27

Visit them and invite them to social gatherings. Often widows feel unwanted in social settings. They see others go out to eat after church while they go home alone. Holidays often find them sitting at home alone because no one thought to inquire about their plans for the holiday meal. Another one of my widowed friends said, *"Sometimes I think widows are ignored, even in the church. We have lost our identities and don't belong anywhere. Everyone thinks we are doing okay, but we aren't."* Widows often put on a smile because they don't want to be a bother. But it is a command of the Word to pay attention and spend time listening and helping them.

Ye shall not afflict any widow, or fatherless child. – Exodus 22:22

141

Do not mistreat the widow and her children. Sometimes widow's children are laughed at and bullied because they may not have the funds to wear nicer clothes and shoes. Proverbs 3:27 instructs us to *Withhold not good from them to whom it is due, when it is in the power of thine hand to do it*. If you see a need and have the means to supply that need, don't mistreat the widow by withholding good things from them. God is watching and will avenge her.

Then Peter arose and went with them. When he was come, they brought him into the upper chamber: and all the widows stood by him weeping, and shewing the coats and garments which Dorcas made, while she was with them. - But Peter put them all forth, and kneeled down, and prayed; and turning him to the body said, Tabitha, arise. And she opened her eyes: and when she saw Peter, she sat up. – Acts 9:39-40

Pray for them. The widows in Joppa had lost Dorcas, their sister who sewed for them. Peter prayed for Dorcas, and God restored her back to her important ministry of providing for the widows. Widows need guidance in making major decisions. Pray for them and help them when possible.

Honour widows that are widows indeed. – 1 Timothy 5:3

Honor them. To honor means to *revere* and hold in *high respect.* Remember their birthdays, anniversaries, and birthdays of their children who are still at home. Recognize acts of service they perform for the church. When my husband first died, someone must have given my birthday and anniversary information to the ladies ministries in the church. During that first year, I received cards on a regular basis. On my first birthday after Ron died, the ladies presented me with a signed card from the ladies in the church as well as a vase filled with a beautiful floral arrangement.

Widows' Responsibility

I have commanded a widow woman there to sustain thee. 1 Kings 17:9

…let thy widows trust in me. Jeremiah 49:11

Now she that is a widow indeed…trusteth in God. I Timothy 5:5

Trust God and the Pastor. A widow woman was commanded to take care of Elijah. Just because a woman becomes a widow does not mean she cannot find a place to work in the Kingdom of God. This widow woman was going to make a final meal for herself and her son and then prepare to die. But when Elijah told her to make him a meal first, she had to exercise trust. The scriptures command the widow to trust.

The woman who threw in her last two mites in the Temple trusted God to provide for future needs, and Jesus commended her for giving her all. He said her all was more than the abundance of those who had given larger sums because she had nothing left for her own needs.

And thou shalt keep the feast of weeks unto the LORD thy God with a tribute of a freewill offering of thine hand, which thou shalt give unto the LORD thy God, according as the LORD thy God hath blessed thee: - And thou shalt rejoice before the Lord thy God, thou, and thy son, and thy daughter, and thy manservant, and thy maidservant, and the Levite that is within thy gates, and the stranger, and the fatherless, and the widow, that are among you, in the place which the Lord thy God hath chosen to place his name there. - Deuteronomy 16:10-11

Do not neglect worship with God's people. God commanded the people, including the *widow*, to *rejoice before the Lord.* He even included those who were dependent upon others for their welfare. Their circumstances or position in life did not exempt them from rejoicing in the Lord. The prophetess, Anna, was eighty-four years old and *served God with fastings and prayers night and day.*

Well reported of for good works; if she have brought up children, if she have lodged strangers, if she have washed the saints' feet, if she have relieved the afflicted, if she have diligently followed every good work.- 1 Timothy 5:10

Industrious. Paul does not say widows are helpless. Many widows have become strong women in the Kingdom of God. Don't allow yourself to lie around the house feeling sorry for yourself because your spouse is gone. Find someone to invest your time into, and much of that heaviness will lift.

And withal they learn to be idle, wandering about from house to house; and not only idle, but tattlers also and busybodies, speaking things which they ought not. – 1 Timothy 5:13

… it is better to marry than to burn. – 1 Corinthians 7:9

Be circumspect and chaste. God is concerned with the conduct of widows. The word circumspect means to be discreet, watchful, guarded, and prudent in behavior. Being single does not give a widow the license to act inappropriately with men or run around being a gossip or busybody.

Maintaining consecration and staying full of the Holy Ghost will help tame the tongue and out-of-control emotions.

God is on your side if you do your part. He has promised to be everything that you need. Thank Him for His promises to you. In Jesus' name!

Scripture References for additional study.

God's Responsibility

Deuteronomy 10:17-19
Deuteronomy 27:19
Psalms 68:5
Psalms 146:9
Proverbs 15:25
Jeremiah 7:5-7
Jeremiah 22:2-4
Jeremiah 49:11
Matthew 23:14
Mark 12:38-40
Luke 7:12-15
Luke 20:46-47

Others' Responsibility

Exodus 22:22
Deuteronomy 14:28-29
Deuteronomy 24:17-19
Deuteronomy 24:20-22
Deuteronomy 26:12-13
Isaiah 1:17
Zechariah 7:10
Luke 18:1-5
Acts 6:1-3
Acts 9:39-40
1 Timothy 5:3-5, 9-10, 16
James 1:27

Widows' Responsibility

Deuteronomy 16:10-15
1 Kings 17:8-24
Mark 23:42-44
Luke 2:36-38
Luke 4:25-26
Luke 21:1-4
1 Corinthians 7:7-9
1 Timothy 5:11-15

About the Author

Pam Eddings has more than twenty years of experience in writing, editing, and proofreading Christian literature, and has assisted in the making of dozens of books and hundreds of articles by both Apostolic and secular writers.

She draws from a lifetime of teaching Sunday School classes, and speaking at seminars, retreats and special events. As a licensed minister and prison Chaplain, she has taught weekly Bible studies since 2003 to thousands of men and women inmates.

Pam is also a skilled singer, musician, and music instructor, and plays active musical and teaching roles in her local Church. She has three sons, three daughters-in-law, two grandsons and four granddaughters. Her home is in Springfield, Missouri.

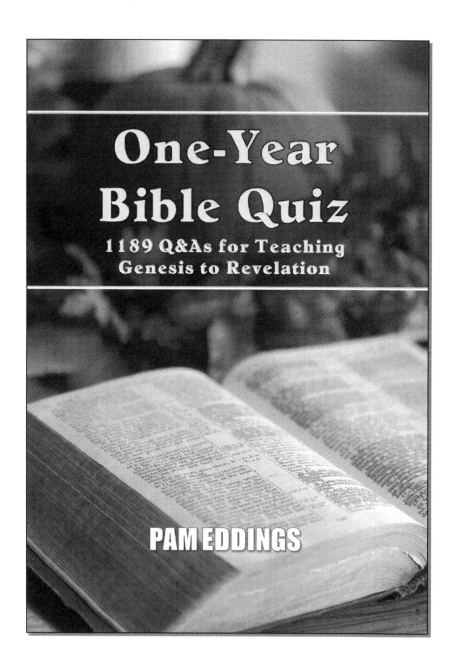

One-Year Bible Quiz

1189 Q&As for Teaching Genesis to Revelation

PAM EDDINGS

One-Year
Bible Quiz

1189 Q&As for Teaching
Genesis to Revelation

In This Book...

One-Year Bible Quiz

The ENTIRE BIBLE has 1189 Chapters. ONE YEAR has 52 weeks.

*Pam Eddings has prepared an extraordinary resource for
Weekly Bible Studies, Sunday School Classes, or Parent-Child Lessons.*

*She has prepared ONE QUESTIONAIRE PER CHAPTER.
All 1189 Q & As are divided equally into 52 WEEKS.*

Each week, you will find just enough
BIBLE QUESTIONS AND ANSWERS
to cover the entire Bible in ONE YEAR.

An OUTSTANDING TEACHING AID!

PAM EDDINGS

Order ONE-YEAR BIBLE QUIZ - 373 pages at
edddingspam@gmail.com

BIBLE

Gems

TO START YOUR DAY

PAM EDDINGS

To order BIBLE GEMS TO START YOUR DAY
email Pam at edddingspam@gmail.com

FOR KIDS

PAM EDDINGS

To order RIGHT STEPS FOR KIDS
email Pam at edddingspam@gmail.com

Godly Women

Saintly Ladies of Yesterday and Today

PAM EDDINGS

To Order Additional Copies of Pam's books:

ONE YEAR BIBLE QUIZ

BIBLE GEMS to Start Your Day

RIGHT STEPS FOR KIDS

GODLY WOMEN – Saintly Ladies of Yesterday and Today

Or

SHE SHALL BE CALLED ABIGAIL – A Widow's Story of God's Love

Please EMAIL her at:

eddingspam@gmail.com

Made in the USA
San Bernardino, CA
19 February 2018